CELTS: LONG JOURl

by

Dennis W. Williams

ISBN - 13: 978-1537063744
ISBN-10: 153706374X

To my wife Pearl

Contents

	Page
INTRODUCTION	**4**
THE CELTS: JOURNEY TO NORTH WALES	**7**
THE AGATHYRSAI	**11**
THE PICTS	**13**
THE MIGRATORY PATH OF THE CIMMERIANS	**15**
LINGUISTICAL LINKS	**23**
HISTORICAL LINKS	**28**
THE DAN TRIBE IN BRITAIN AND EUROPE	**34**
CULTURES	**40**
ARCHAEOLOGICAL ANALYSES	**47**
THE BRYTHONIC	**52**
THE VOTADINI	**55**
THE CELTS	**58**
THE ROMANS	**59**
CUNEDDA - Father of the Welsh Nation	**64**
OWAIN GWYNEDD King of Gwynedd	**69**
OWAIN GLYNDWR **The last native born Prince of Wales**	**73**

Bibliography & Acknowledgements   87

MAPS:

Map 1. Path of early Indo-European languages   17

Map 2. Ancient Assyrian Empire (858-627 B.C.)   19

Map 3. The Indo-European Speaking Peoples   25

Map 4. Cradle of Indo-European   26

Map 5. Bell-Beaker Culture Distribution   41

PHOTOGRAPHS

Caer Drewyn Hill-Fort, Corwen, North Wales   61

Royal great seal of Owain Glyndwr   73

Tapered granite cross shaft   84

Lintel above the door   85

ILLUSTRATIONS
Figure 1. Proto-Indo-European Language Group   8

CELTIC BLESSING / BENDITH GELTAIDD   86

INDEX   91

Front cover design: Red Dragon of Wales and Coat of Arms of Cunedda Wledig by Dennis Williams

Introduction

We are of the Steppes of Europe, of ancient Sumeria, of Mesopotamia; we were part of the creation of the Indus Valley civilization, the earliest known urban culture of the Indian subcontinent; we were the Cimmerians; we became the Brythonic; we came to speak the oldest spoken language in Europe; we were to become the Votadini, ultimately becoming of Edeyrnion.

The connection between the people of North Wales and the Manaw Gododdin area in the region of East Lothian in Scotland has long been known by historians. On the way to Edinburgh to discover a little more of this tribal association there is a slight detour to the ancient civilizations of Persia (Iran), Mesopotamia (Iraq), as well as that of the Indus Valley, a Bronze-Age civilization extending from what is today Northeast Afghanistan to Pakistan and Northwest India.

One of the fastest growing pastimes, indeed to many a profession no less, is that of genealogy. Tracing family ancestry is both a pleasurable and rewarding pursuit, one that nowadays can be done just as easily over the Internet as searching Parish and County Records, although the latter, at some stage of a family history research is essential.

In tracing family ancestry it is inevitable that at some stage there will be the inability to create a positive link between one generation and the previous one. This invariably leads to guesswork and often erroneous results. However, now and again fortune smiles her face with transparency, results appear not as misguided as first thought bringing about some transformation to that which we are seeking.

And so it is with searching tribal ancestry, that often there is a lack of order of both events and information leading to much disarray. As with tracing family history, there comes a time when seemingly, there is nothing but a vacuum and no written records available.

The Indo-European migration is one of the most important events in the history of mankind, following which they were distributed over a larger portion of the earth than any other language or ethnic group. As one modern-day journey commences an ancient epic journey unfolds.

The first Indo-European groups of wanderers headed due west to settle Anatolia and the Mediterranean basin. Other groups remained firmly on terra-firma traversing the Caspian Sea area in a counterclockwise direction. Remaining tribes turned west when they reached the Russian steppe, entering Europe by way of the Ukraine. Eastern bound groups found their way to the Indus Valley.

The groups of peoples linking our past are those of the Agathyrsai, the Picts, the Scythians and, most consistent with findings, the Cimmerians and the Votadini. The Cimmerians were fair hair and fair skinned, first located in southern Ukraine but numerous texts presume their ancestral roots to be farther east.

There is no doubt that we were part of the great Indo-European expansion, the greatest migration in human history. Our earliest settlements on these islands were in the north of ancient Britain of what is now Scotland, the Cimmerians settling in the area of Manaw Gododdin in East Lothian. Is there a connection here with Mannai, an ancient country in northwestern Iran, south of Lake Urmia where at one stage of the transmigration the Cimmerians were located?

According to Virgil, the Roman's task was to govern the world under their dominion, *'to establish civilisation where there was peace, to grant mercy where there was submission and to crush by war where there was defiance'*. During their occupancy of ancient Britain their army numbered tens of thousands; given that they remained on these shores until the 5th century A.D we must accept that their members intermingled with those of the indigenous groups, therefore we must not doubt Roman contribution to that of Edeyrnion's populace!

At the same time as the Romans commenced their departure from these parts an army of Votadini Celts were advancing from the north of Britain towards what is now North Wales. What was the purpose of this manoeuvre and who was the leader of this army of Celts?

To most of us, Old King Cole was a mythical character in nursery rhyme. It appears he may well have been the grandfather of Edeyrnion. The importance of archaeological and linguistic evidence are both vital, and despite the advances made by DNA technology, consideration is also given to the application of strontium isotope and oxygen isotope analysis. Archaeological findings have linked us to a group of peoples known to history as Cimmerians, and Scythians.

The complexity of languages is apparent and yet there are many clear cases of convergence in the development of well-documented languages.

Strange as it may sound, but how was it that the Asiatic Society in Bengal came to discover the link between the modern-day Welsh language and other branches of the Indo-European group of languages? I have attempted to highlight these links using examples from ancient Sumerian, Hebrew and Sanskrit in addition to a number of Proto-Indo-European words. The Australian historian Yair Davidii states that of the modern-day languages, the one closest to ancient Hebrew is Welsh.

In importing copper technology to ancient Britain including Wales, the Beaker folk also introduced improved methods of farming and may also have introduced an Indo-European language to these islands. Despite their arrival on these shores dating approximately to 2,000 years B.C. some of their farming methods were more advanced than those of the Romans.

Whilst Edeyrnion cannot lay claim to Owain Gwynedd, his connections with the area are significant enough to include a chapter as it was on Caer Drewyn in Corwen that he, together with an assembly of a great Welsh army plus the inclement weather, forced Henry II into a retreat from the Berwyn Mountains.

The death in the 13th century of the Prince of Northern Powys resulted in Edeyrnion's most famous historical link - that of Owain Glyndwr. A wealth of evidence survive in many Manuscript's of lifelong events relating to Owain, yet despite this, little is known of his resting place. Some clues suggest this could well be within the grounds of the Church of St Mael and St Sulien in Corwen. However, recent research discovered papers that may give us the answer to where the great man died.

We, the people of Edeyrnion, were part of the Indo-European expansion, of that there is no doubt. What is unclear however is the full path of that transmigration and most of the events which took place during its course of some 2,500 to 3,000 years. What I sincerely hope the result of the research undertaken gives us, is at the very least an outline of our ancient past, and at best the evidence to enrich this with detail.

Researching, locating and recording the facts are always the easiest; making the facts come together in a coherent story is by far the most difficult part because there is nothing about human lives over centuries that is coherent. History is not made of a few big things but of many small things.

As always there is much which I owe to many people for their help and kindness during the gathering of material for this publication. And to my wife Pearl I thank her for always being there.

THE CELTS: LONG JOURNEY TO WALES

We shall not cease from exploration
And the end of all our exploring
Will be to arrive where we started
And know the place for the first time.

T.S. Eliot - Little Gidding (1942)

One of the increasingly popular and growing pastimes is that of genealogy, our fascination with the past creating great interest in tracing family descent. On a similar theme is that of tracing our tribal descent albeit a much larger scale research.

Having said that it appears first hand to imagine that tracing ancestral tribes would be easier due to the wealth of available written works whereas in fact these are limited and factual verification often proves difficult. As with tracing family line, the further back we wish to go, we discover records and written historical text are both limited.

Celts have descended from the Indo-European group of peoples; more recent evidence places the probable origin of the Indo-European language in western Asia.

This quest to discover links with our historical and ancestral past and some frequently asked questions by human geographers and historians alike are (i) who were our ancestors?; (ii) where did we come from?; (iii) what brought us here?, and (iv) why are we here? To answer these questions will surprisingly and, hopefully interestingly, take us back in time to about 4000 - 3000 B.C. and a route of some 12,000 miles during which time our ancestors embraced the most ancient of civilizations.

The number of languages spoken today depends partly on our definition of language; leaving out minor dialects it is estimated that there are still around 3000 different languages in current use with at least another 4000 that have gone out of use.

Language is the essential linking device in human cultures, enabling members of a group to communicate freely with each other. It also becomes a barrier when members of one language group cannot linguistically communicate with members of another language group. If two persons or two groups of different origins attempt to communicate with each other then language becomes an immediate obstacle. In time the two groups will develop a new word list and signs to bridge the gap. These words will comprise of existing vocabulary from both groups and a fusion of words from both sets together with a sub-set of entirely new words.

The origin and dispersal of languages illustrate clearly a second theme in cultural geography and the most important question we must ask to understand this process concerns the relation of one language to another. Many accept current circumstances as a matter of fact with little interest, whilst others display a great desire with our history and concern for how we arrived at where we are today. At various intervals we need to discover some pointers establishing details to our past history.

Extensive linguistic research has revealed that many different languages seem to have emerged from a common stock and the distilling out of the main language groups, linguistic origins and differentiation was a slow process over thousands of years. Changes over a much shorter period are noticeable in dialects within a language, but languages themselves are stable enough to provide useful spatial signals of the migrational history of various groups, see Figure 1 - Indo-European Language Map.

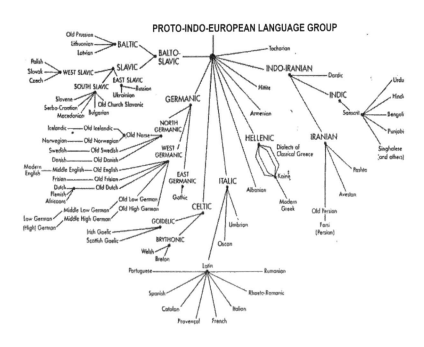

Figure 1. Indo-European Language Map

During the period c.4000 B.C. to c.3000 B.C the earliest division of tongues within the Proto-Indo-European language slowly started its refinement into two dialectal groups, one of which included the Celtic groups from which the Welsh language emanated.

Many latterday historians have written indicating our origin was of Mediterranean stock from the Iberian peninsula. However, a closer understanding of the migrational process of peoples and languages may help to establish our earliest known descendants to have originated much farther east, probably Persia (modern-day Iran), Mesopotamia (modern-day Iraq) and possibly as far east as the Indian sub-continent.

Historians Thomas V. Gamkrelidze and V.V. Ivanov state that the linguistic translocation of the Indo-European homeland from northern Europe to Asia Minor requires drastic revisions in theories about the paths along which the Indo-European languages must have spread across Eurasia. Thus, the hypothetical Aryans who were said to have borne the so-called Aryan, or Indo-Iranian language from Europe to India, turn out to be the real Indo-Iranians who made the more plausible migration from Asia Minor around the northern slopes of the Himalaya Mountains and down through modern Afghanistan to settle in India. Europe is seen therefore as the destination, rather than the source, of Indo-European migration.

Generations of archaeologists and linguists have thus far excavated and deciphered manuscripts in close to a dozen ancient languages from sites in modern Turkey and as far east as Tocharia, in modern Turkestan. Their observations, together with new ideas in pure linguistic theory, have made it necessary to revise the canons of linguistic evolution. (see paragraph on linguistic links to Welsh language).

The Indo-European migration is one of the most important events in the history of mankind. Around 2300 - 2000 B.C the Indo-Europeans were to be found only in the Caucasus mountains; after the migration they were distributed over a larger portion of the earth than any other language/racial group. However, it was also an undocumented migration; it happened so early that today's Indo-Europeans have no record, not even legends, of their ancestors' journey. Historians have resorted to archaeology and language comparison to deduce the great migrational path.

The first group or groups of wanderers headed due west to settle Anatolia and the Mediterranean basin. These seagoing pioneers became the Hittites, the Greeks, and possibly the "Mediterranean" peoples of Italy and Spain. Other groups remained firmly on terra-firma, traversing the Caspian Sea area in a counter clockwise direction. As they did so, individual tribes broke off from the main body, to become the Indo-Iranian ethnic groups: Medes, Persians, Kurds, Parthians, Scythians, Afghans, and the various groups now found in Pakistan and north India. The remaining tribes turned west when they reached the Russian steppe, entering Europe by way of the Ukraine. As the area they spread across grew larger, communications between the tribes failed, and individual dialects became languages. A result of this was, that when the Indo-Europeans finally settled down in western and central Europe, they were not one nation but many: Teutons, Celts, Slavs, Balts, and so on.

The diversity of human cultures and their innate complexity is staggering and most scholarly research has long since done away with the notion that culture is a small number of well defined and simplistic sets of values. It is perhaps best summarized by saying that culture describes patterns of learned human behaviour that form templates by which ideas and images can be transferred from one generation to another, or from one group to another. From this we can therefore presume that the transfer of these templates is not through biological means but that the main imprinting forces in cultural transfers are symbolic, with language playing a particularly important role. Finally, the transfer process is always incomplete as the culture of the group is always many times larger than the culture of the individual.

What I have attempted to do is take a line establishing links between various nations/tribes which are both linguistic and symbolical; linguistic links will exhibit vocabulary similarities; symbolical links would display similarities within cultures as diverse as agriculture practices, pottery artistic designs, burial patterns etc. and the greatest research tools available offered by archaeologist's in the form of oxygen isotope analysis, strontium isotope analysis and DNA analysis. Searching for evidence to establish connections between our current circumstances - nation, language, culture etc. - and those of our ancestors - has proved a difficult task with the scarcity of written texts together with the passage of time between these various points. The main groups of peoples linking our past are those of the Agathyrsai, the Picts, the Scythians, and, most consistent with findings, the Cimmerians and the Votadini.

THE AGATHYRSAI

Although it is not with any certainty as to when the Picts arrived on these shores, some evidence suggests c.760 B.C., we do know that they colonized the area of northern Britain in what is today the district of East Lothian in Scotland and in particular Edinburgh. The name Edinburgh derives from Dineidin, mentioned in a Welsh poem of the 6th century, 'Y Gododdin' (Aneirin), Din or Dun being Celtic for fort and Eidin or Edin is the ancient name for hill. The Saxon for dun is burgh.

The work of Yair Davidii *(Lost Israelite Identity)* details the Picts' artistic use of vegetation and linking this to examples of it on Assyrian and Persian bas reliefs. This discovery, Davidii explains, is that the artistic style of the Picts confirms their eastern origins and concerning this style it has been remarked that: *"The animals which include fish, birds, bulls, boars, and deer are executed with vigour and economy in a style common to the barbarians from northern Britain to the borders of China".* In other words, the Picts used the Scythian art style. This style continued to be employed by the "Barbarians" (such as Angles, Saxons, and Franks) who emerged from Scythia as well as by the Picts who had migrated from the same regions. The fundamental elements of this style and its means of execution may be traced back to the area of ancient Israel.

The Anglo-Saxon historian Bede made the claim that the Picts were Scythian, maintaining that their descent is common with that of the Celts from the Albani or Gentes Scitiae (People of Scythia), and this according to Davidii is consistent with descent from the Agathyrsai. The Agathyrsai came to northern Britain from Scythia and the Romans suggested they had crossed the sea to become forefathers of the Picts, though what proportion they actually composed of this Tribe is uncertain. The Agathyrsai at various stages had been reported of in different places: - as being in the Pontus (in northeast Turkey) on the Black Sea shore just west of the Caucasus Mountains; - in the north on the Baltic Sea shore according to Ptolemy; - and, under the name of Akatziri, in the north, to the south of Estonia near the Baltic Seashore. The Lithuanian archaeologist, Marija Gimbutas' hypothesis concerning the people who produced the North Pontic culture states that c.2000 - 800 B.C *"the Cimmerian people were located between the lower Danube and Caucasus Mountains".* The region of the Caucasus was inhabited by "a confusion of tribes about whom it is truer to be vague than precise, such as the Cimmerians, the Sarmatians, and those Scythians who came into contact with the Assyrian Empire by 1,000 B.C." Indeed, as with any other ethnogenesis, it is always difficult to tell what was the exact ethnic origin of the Central Asian steppes or European peoples, but there is no doubting the role the Indo-European people were to play in the creation of European identity thus laying down the founding stone of European civilisation. Unfortunately, the picture, however defined, gets more blurry as time periods overlap.

THE PICTS

The Picts also included elements from other tribes who had merged with them. Eventually they became an amalgamation of Israelite elements who from several directions and at different stages merged on the same areas. They used a type of horse harness known from the Don River region in southern Scythia. In the Pict area of northern Britain there was a river named the Don and, according to Davidii, another called the Gadie (*in fact there are two rivers Don, one which rises in Yorkshire and the second which Davidii is concerned with, rises in the Grampians, but I cannot trace a river Gadie within the British Isles - although a River Gade rises in the Chiltern Hills*) so this may well be the one he refers to. These names (i.e. "Don" and "Gadie") are traceable to Scythia, the Goths and to the Israelite Tribes of Dan and Gad. The Pict symbols included a mirror and comb and the sun appearing overhead of a sailing ship. Similar symbols have been reported from Scandinavia and are known from studies of ancient Egypt. The Picts also used an elephant symbol and a serpent-like figure. Examples of Pictish art are found on more than a hundred monuments scattered all over the north of Scotland though especially concentrated in the Classical Pict area of the northeast.

But most of what is now known as Assyrian art as well as much of the ancient Persian was actually directly produced by Israelite and Phoenician craftsmen and is a development of the "Syrian" area. It appeared after the Israelites had been exiled and was promoted by Israelite and "Syrian" craftsmen. This has been proven by signatures in Hebrew on articles of art found in Assyrian excavations. This was the same style later to be found on Pict monuments in northern Britain as well as in Ireland.

The Agathyrsai (Akatziri) were to form the nucleus of the Khazar people who were located in southern Russia and converted to Judaism. Caucasian Subarian traditions maintain that the Agathyrsians originated in Assur, i.e. there exists a tradition that the Agathyrsai came from Assyria and this is consistent with their having been Israelites who were exiled to Assyria and re-settled by the Assyrians on the fringes of their Empire.

The Khazars were described by Arab authors as consisting of three types: 1. A dark haired, dark-complexioned one similar to Hindus; 2. A dark haired, and light pale-skinned one, and 3. A red haired, blue-eyed, large limbed, wild countenanced, heavy moving one. All three of these complexions (with some modification due to climate and intermarriages) were to be found amongst the Celtic tribes of Britain.

13

The Khazars were also linked with the Goths. The Caledonians of northern Britain confederated with the Picts and they too were regarded as a north European group. The Caledonians were related to the Votadini of North Wales who had come from northern Britain. Both groups descend from Gilead son of Machir of Menasseh. The Picts who came from Scythia and were descended from the Agathyrsai are often confused with indigenous peoples in northern Britain with whom they may have amalgamated and to whom the name "Pict" may also have been applied to at some stage or other. The Picts are archaeologically distinguished by their way of drawing animals and by certain symbols they employed.

According to the historian D.A. MacKenzie, *the Picts were never very numerous and formed a military elite that ultimately came to dominate all of northern Britain*. The name "Picti" is first found in Eumenius c.296 A.D. but Sidonius Apollinaris assigned them an earlier time around that of Julius Caesar.

At the same time as the invading Picts supposedly arrived in northern Britain, the Cimmerians, according to some historians, despite their removal from the Pontic/Russian steppes by the Scythians, were now in the process of invading Europe and Asia.

THE MIGRATORY PATH OF THE CIMMERIANS

Mesopotamia (Iraq), Persia (Iran), Ukraine, Britain

The Cimmerians, fair hair and fair skinned, are mentioned in various texts and publications which first locate them in southern Ukraine - whether this was their ancestral or trasmigrational home it is difficult to establish, but numerous texts presume their ancestral roots to be Mesopotamia (modern-day Iraq). With some certainty however we do know that their historical passage from hereon was part of the Indo-European expansion. Linguistically they are usually regarded as Iranian, or at least to have had an Iranian ruling class. They probably did live in the area north of the Black Sea, but attempts to define their original homeland more precisely by archaeological means, or even to fix the date of their expulsion from their country by the Scythians, have not so far been completely successful.

Is there sufficient evidence provided to establish that Celtic peoples could possibly consider themselves descended from the Cimmerians as some of their ethnic names seem to bear out this belief, i.e. Cymru - Wales and Cymro - Welshman, or is all this too fragmented? or too easy to make such assumptions?

What becomes clear is that the Cimmerians do move on - ancient legends about the "People of the Flood" were known as Cimmerians, who occupied areas around the Black Sea. A number of texts show that these Cimmerians are the same as the Mesopotamian Sumerians and Samarians, and that the name Cimmeri is Indo-European.

Cimmerians & Mesopotamia

Cimmerians - also known as Cimmer, Cimmerian, Cimbri, Cimbris, Crimea, Chomari, Cymric, Cymry, Cumber, Gamir, Gommer, Gomeri, Gomeria, Gimmer, Gimmerai, Gimirrai, Gimirraya, Kimmer, Kimmeroi, Kimirraa, Kumri, Umbri

Cimmerians were a nomadic people who moved about the Pontic Steppes and, having risen first in Mesopotamia, migrated across the Median Plateau of Iran into Central Asia where they lived for many centuries. Some archaeologists divide Cimmerians into a Western (Thracian-Sumerian) and Eastern (Kizil-Koba Colchis) group. Using this division, archaeologists begin to get more accurate dates going back to c. 2000 BC.

The Cimmerians are traced to the Indus Valley in India whose civilization was destroyed in 1550 B.C. and both India and Iran were occupied by these fair skinned Cimmerians from Mesopotamia. It is not clear however what became of this group - did they return westwards or did they remain on this vast continent and eventually disappeared either by extinction or ethnic assimilation?

Cimmerians are the earliest known inhabitants of the Crimea. Strabo writes: *"Cimmerians once possessed great power in the Bosporus and is why it is called the Cimmerian Bosporus."* The name Crimea is derived from Cimmeria. Cimmerian tribes, Celts and Gauls, because of inhospitable climate and pressure of migrating Scythian tribes, began to leave the area around the Crimea. An uncoordinated migration began about 1200 BC in two groups to the regions south of the Black Sea, one moving east and the other moving west, establishing settlements on the way. One group crossed the Pontic Bosporus, moving toward the Hittite kingdom from the west, while the other group came from the northeast through the Caucasus and converged on the Hittite kingdom.

They migrated back through the Caucasus from the 12th - 8th century BC. Some authorities identify them with "Thraco-Cimmerian" remains of the 8th-7th century BC found in the southwestern Ukraine and in central Europe.

Herodotus reports that Cimmerians were driven out of the Black Sea region over the Caucasus into Mesopotamia by Scythians. In 634 B.C., Cimmerians came to the region around Lake Van (Eastern Turkey). This again is consistent with maps displaying the path of the Indo-European languages.

Map 1. Path of migration of the Pro-Indo-European languages.

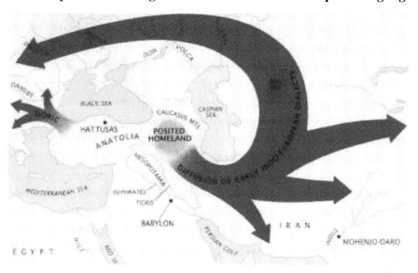

Their journey continues as shown in Map 1 (Migration of Proto-Indo-Europeans). This clearly displays the path branching in four directions - (i) south to Iran; (ii) eastwards to the Indus Valley; (iii) north-eastwards towards Afghanistan, Pakistan and north India and (iv) the fourth branch is the counterclockwise route northwards encompassing the Caspian-Sea area. Then once having reached the Russian-steppes the path takes a westerly direction, and this appears, in all probability, to be the one that the Cimmerians journeyed. Some would say this is pure speculation but as this route entered the Ukraine and the Cimmerians were at one stage located there, then substance is added to the theory.7

In the publication '*The Exile*', Yair Davidii mentions the original Twelve Tribes of Israel had split into two kingdoms. Two tribes comprising "Judah" were in the south, and the ten tribes of "Israel" were in the north. The Ten Northern Tribes were entirely taken away by the Assyrians to places in northern Mesopotamia, to the Caucasus area and to eastern Iran.

Archaeological findings enable the identification of these places of re-settlement. Shortly after the exile and re-settlement every one of the said places became a centre for a group of peoples who then appeared for the first time. They are known to history as the Cimmerians, Scythians, and Guti or Goths and these entities were (at least in part) the Lost Ten Tribes of Israel!

The bulk of the Israelites had been exiled in the period 730-710 BC, possibly earlier. In about 707 B.C. a people named "Gimirae" were

17

reported from the region of Mannaie These are the Cimmerians. It is worth mentioning Mannae and the posible connection here with Manaw Gododdin, the Latin name referring to both the region and the Brythonic people located in the area of northern Britain of Manaw Gododdin.

Mannae was an ancient country in northwestern Iran, south of Lake Urmia. During the period of its existence in the early 1st millennium BC, Mannae was surrounded by three major powers: Assyria, Urartu, and Media. The Mannaeans are first recorded in the annals of the Assyrian king Shalmaneser III (reigned 858–824 BC) and are last mentioned in Urartu by Rusa II (reigned 685–645 BC) and in Assyria by Esarhaddon (reigned 680–669 BC). The Cimmerians, in their transmigration were located here as can be seen in Map 2 of Ancient Assyria .

I cannot be more precise as to the date they were established here but further substance is added to the link between the Cimmerians who were at one time located in Mannae and later at Manaw Gododdin, the area of ancient northern Britain where they eventually settled, thereby linking our ancestry to that of the Cimmerians and their origin within the middle-east.

Cimmerians were also referred to as "Amuru" meaning Amorite, but in Assyrian usage the expression meant "Dweller of the Land of Israel" or "Previous Dweller of the Land of Israel and/or Syria". These Cimmerians, via the Balkans and Danube valley, eventually reached Gaul, the British Isles, and Scandinavia. They became the major factor in "Celtic" civilization.

After their first appearance, the Scythians and Cimmerians are recognizable as distinct entities though, in effect, both bodies were combinations of Scythians proper, of Goths, and of Cimmerians in varying proportions. From the north the Scythians were eventually to continue westward into Europe.

The ancient Cimmerians, to whom Assyrian chronicles refer as "Gimirrai", a barbaric people wandering between the Caspian Sea and Anatolia invaded Lydia. Cimmerians had to emigrate towards Western Europe, where they finally settled and became known in history as the Celtic peoples, or Gallic by the Romans. Their ethnic name, Cymru, is present in many toponyms in different regions and countries, as Cymru (Wales), Umbria, Northumbria, Cumberland, etc; while their Roman name is present in others like Galica, Galicia, Britain, etc.

Historian Van Loon identified a people in north Armenia (near Lake Leninkan close to the border with Iberia in Georgia) named Isqi-Gulu as Scythian. Isqi-Gulu is the equivalent of Isaac-Golu! i.e. the Exiles of Isaac since Golu in Hebrew connotes exiled. Variations of the name Isaac were applied to the Scythians who in many respects were identical with, or identified as, the Cimmerians. A city named after the Cimmerians and called Gymrias or Gamir was to be found in the Isqi-Gulu area. This city was later referred to as Kumayri (present day Gyumrai) and this name strongly suggests a Cimmerian presence as well as being an alternate Assyrian pronunciation of Omri which was the name they gave to northern Israel. *(See Map 2: Ancient Assyrian Empire, 858-627 B.C.)*

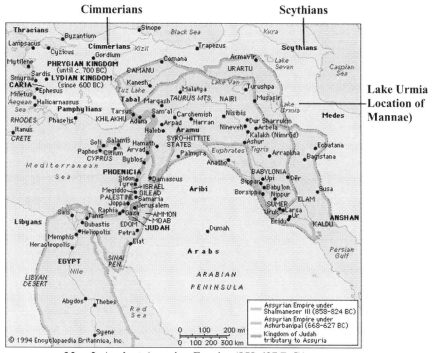

Map 2. Ancient Assyrian Empire (858-627 B.C.)
showing the location of the Cimmerians,
Scythians and Mannae.

Cimmerian Archaeological Discoveries

It has been suggested that the introduction of gray and gray-black pottery into western Iran from the northeast, signaling the commencement of the Iron Age, is the archaeological manifestation of a pattern of a gradual movement of Iranians from east to west. The case, whilst not offering conclusive proof, is certainly considered as a reasonable reading of the combined evidence. Thus, the argument links these archaeological patterns with the Iranian migration and with their infiltration westward along the major routes to Europe and eventually to ancient Britain.

The avenues by which eastern concepts reached Europe have never been established with certainty. Some have regarded the steppe nomads as the means of transmission. These undoubtedly were the Cimmerians. The picture is indeed complex and it is believed that 'Cimmerians' is a term that covers a number of groups with different origins. They do appear to have contributed to the spread of naturalistic animal art. The Celtic interpretation of such art seems to have resulted in forms that are much less formal and rigid, and given the known lifestyle of nomadic tribes, an indeterminate picture without cohesion or unity is precisely what would be expected in tracing the influences of such an intangible phenomenon as their style or taste.

However, archaeologist's, having looked closely at Celtic art and artefacts of various periods have determined some elements that can be claimed as coming from the east via the nomadic tribes which most certainly would have included the Cimmerians.

The Historian Tamara Talbot Rice confirms that *"the Scythians did not become a recognizable national entity much before the eighth century B.C. and that by the seventh century B.C. they had established themselves firmly in southern Russia. Assyrian documents place their appearance there (between the Black Sea and the Caspian Sea) in the time of King Sargon (722-705 B.C.) a date that closely corresponds with that of the establishment of the first group of Scythians and Cimmerians in southern Russia"*.

In his book *"The Ancient World of the Celts"* historian Peter Ellis notes; *"At the start of the first millennium BC, a civilization which had developed from its Indo-European roots around the headwaters of the Rhine, the Rhone and the Danube suddenly erupted in all directions through Europe. Greek merchants, first encountering them in the sixth century BC, called them Keltoi and Galatai. Today we generally identify them as Celts"*. Many of these so-called barbarian tribes were racially and culturally related and the language of the related tribes can be traced to a common parent language - Indo-European.

They were adept at travelling the hub, or nexus, rivers north of the Mediterranean Sea including the Rhine, Danube, Seine and Rhone, rivers which all come close together. This hub was once a key link to the communication and trade flowing between the Atlantic, Nordic-Baltic, eastern Black Sea and Mediterranean trading zones. It was a major gateway to all of Europe. Historian Samuel Lysons spoke of *"the Cimmerians seeming to be the same people as the Gauls or Celts under a different name"* (John Henry and James Parker, *Our British Ancestors: Who and What Were They?).*

Anne Kristensen, a respected Danish linguistic scholar, recently reached the conclusion that the Cimmerians (who later became known as the Celts) can positively be identified as the deported Israelites. In the beginning of her research Dr. Kristensen was sceptical and subscribed to the traditional theory that Cimmerians were "Aryan" tribes the Scythians had scared out of the north. But further investigation into the Assyrian sources she found the Cimmerians first appeared in history in 714 B.C. in the region of Iran south of Armenia where the kings of Assyria had settled many of the deported Israelites. She came to the conclusion that the Gimira, or Cimmerians, represented at least a part of the lost 10 tribes of Israel.

"There is scarcely reason, any longer, to doubt the exciting and astonishing assertion propounded by the students of the Ten Tribes that the Israelites deported from Bit Humria, of the House of 'Omri, are identical with the Gimirraja of the Assyrian sources. Everything indicates that Israelite deportees did not vanish from the picture but that, abroad, under new conditions, they continued to leave their mark on history" (*Who Were the Cimmerians, and Where Did They Come From?: Sargon II, the Cimmerians, and Rusa I,* translated from the Danish by Jorgen Laessoe, The Royal Danish Academy of Sciences and Letters, No. 57, 1988, pp. 126-127).

During the late eighth century B.C., records from the Caucasian kingdom of Urartu, which controlled the northern reaches of the Euphrates River, also noted the appearance of a group called Cimmerians.

The book 'From the Lands of the Scythians' explains: *"... Two groups, Cimmerians and Scythians, seem to be referred to in Urartean and Assyrian texts, but it is not always clear whether the terms indicate two distinct peoples or simply mounted nomads ... Beginning in the second half of the eighth century B.C., Assyrian sources refer to nomads identified as the Cimmerians; other Assyrian sources say these people were present in the land of the Mannai (or Mannea, south of Lake Urmia) and in Cappadocia for a hundred years (that is, about 750 to 650 B.C.), and record their advances into Asia Minor and Egypt".*

The Assyrians used Cimmerians in their army as mercenaries; a legal document of 679 B.C. refers to an Assyrian 'commander of the Cimmerian regiment'; but in other Assyrian documents they are called *"the seed of runaways who know neither vows to the gods nor oaths"*.

It is also worth noting that Assyrian crown prince Sennacherib wrote a secret intelligence report that archaeologists found during the excavation of the royal archives at Nineveh. Sennacherib's report passed on news from his spies that Cimmerian nomads had invaded Urartu and had defeated their forces. On the strength of that report the Assyrians made preparations to invade their northern rival, Urartu, which they successfully accomplished in 714 B.C.

Considerable evidence connects the Celts of Europe with the Cimmerians who fled from the Near East to Asia Minor at the time the armies of Babylon were conquering the Assyrian Empire. From Asia Minor the Cimmerians migrated by way of the Danube River into Europe, where they became known as the Celts. Many historians have concluded that the Celts, Cimmerians and Scythians have a common background.

Historians and archaeologists report that during the second half of the first millennium B.C. the area of Europe north of the Mediterranean world shared two related cultures. From the British Isles to the headwaters of the Danube to the eastern fringe of the Alps existed what historians label as the Hallstatt Celtic culture and, later, the La Tène Celtic culture.

But further east, occupying a vast area of Eastern Europe, was the strong horse-centred traditional Scythe culture based on a way of life suited to grasslands rather than mountains and forests. Each of these provided ideas and inspiration for the other. According to the archaeological evidence, the two groups freely intermarried.

The separate Celtic, Cimmerian and Scythian cultures interacted with each other much like modern Britain and America. Each was adapted to the geography of its own region. But the people themselves interacted as if they shared an ancestry. Archaeologists have uncovered some remarkable sites that demonstrate how closely these peoples worked with each other.

Dr Jeaninne Davis-Kimbell links her Scythian discoveries with women in the Celtic sphere, drawing us back to the fact that the Celts descended from the Cimmerians who, it is commonly admitted are archaeologically indistinguishable from the Scythians.

LINGUISTICAL LINKS

Following is a short list of Ancient Sumerian links to the modern-day Welsh language.

English	Sumerian	Welsh
father	ada	tad or tada;
Mother	ama	mam
Drive	gur	gyrru
Eye	igi	llygaid
Bear	az	arth
Boil	bir	berwi
Host	lu	llu
Water	ur	dwr
River	aba	afon - aber (mouth of river)
Hundred		
Weight	cantar	cant (hundredweight)
Myself	ni	yfi

Proto-Indo-European Language Links

In addition to the above a number of Proto-Indo-European words are known to have links to the modern-day Welsh:-

English	Indo-European	Welsh	
Dog	kwon	ci (singular)	cwn (plural)
Lamb	owi	oen	
Yoke	ieuo	iau	
Sea	mori	môr	
Honey	mélit	mêl	
mead	médhu	medd	
barley	bhares	barlys	
plough	arae	aradr	
farrow	porko	perchyll	
God	Deiw-os	Duw	

That such similarities exist after a period of some 5000 years appears

23

incredible - the small sample must be emphasised as the word lexicon I researched was a very small base, it strongly exhibits the probability of a link between the ancient civilization of Sumeria and Wales.

The source language, generally called "Proto-Indo-European", was spoken some 6,500 years ago according to J. P. Mallory. It is from c.4000 B.C. to c. 3000 B.C that Greek, Thracian and Indo-Iranian form as independent languages. At about the same time the earliest division of tongues within the Proto-Indo-European language slowly started its refinement into two dialectal groups, one of which included the Celtic groups from which the Welsh language emanated.

Language similarities (see above) between the modern Welsh and the ancient Proto-Indo-European Language show up in animal names such as (dogs - kwón - cwn), (lambs - owi - oen) and sea was (mori - môr). There were vehicles with wheels for which I cannot establish any links but these were pulled by teams joined by (yokes - yugó - ieuo). Honey (mélit - mêl) was known, and it probably formed the basis of an alcoholic drink (mead - médhu - medd). The Indo-Europeans practiced agriculture and the cultivation of cereals. as well as (barley - bhares - barlys), (plough - arae - aradr) and (farrow - porko- perchyll). We can reconstruct with certainty the word for "god," (deiw-os - Duw). These link the Indo-European to the Picts and the ancient Brythonic (Welsh).

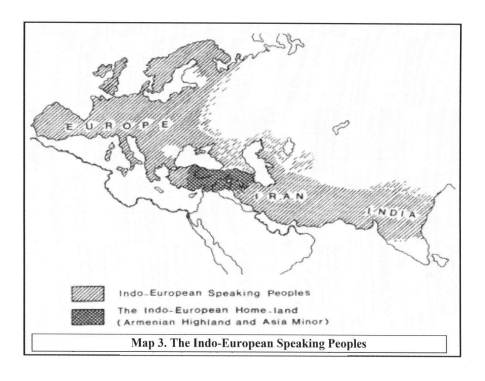

Map 3. The Indo-European Speaking Peoples

Map 4. Cradle of Indo-European

SEMITIC LINKS TO THE WELSH LANGUAGE

Semitic influences in Indo European:-

English	Semitic	Indo-European	Welsh
Bull	tawr	tauro	tarw
Goat	gadj	ghaid	gafr

The same lexicons (word lists) were borrowed by Indo-Europeans from other Afroasiatic, Caucasian, Urartian, Hurrian, Sumerian languages. Building on this, Gamkrelidze and Ivanov believe that the Indo-European homeland lay in Northern Mesopotamia (Iraq), between the Caucasus and Anatolia, in what is now Kurdistan and Armenia.

Early studies of Indo-European languages focused on those most familiar to the original European researchers: the Italic, Celtic, Germanic, Baltic and Slavic families. Affinities between these and the "Aryan" languages spoken in faraway India were noticed by European travellers as early as the 16th century. That they might all share a common ancestor was first proposed in 1786 by Sir William Jones, an English jurist and student of Eastern cultures during a lecture to the Royal Asiatic Society of Bengal. He thus launched what came to be known as the Indo-European hypothesis, which served as the principal stimulus to the founders of historical linguistics in the 18th century (1786). (A branch of Indo-European had been identified almost eighty years earlier (1707) by Edward Lhuyd, curator of the Ashmolean Museum in Oxford who recognised the relationship between Welsh, Irish, Scottish, Gaelic and Breton

ROMANY LANGUAGE

The Slovenian scholar Franz von Miklosich whose work in comparative linguistics estimates that the Romany language separated from related North Indian languages about AD1000, and that modern Romany dialects all over the world have been classified according to their European originals, of which there are thirteen: Greek, Romanian, Hungarian, Czecho-Slovak, German, Polish, Russian, Finnish, Scandinavian, Italian, Serbo-Croatian, Welsh, and Spanish. According to Miklosich the vocalic (vowel) and consonantal systems of all Romany dialects are clearly derived from Sanskrit and adds that the numerous languages of the Indo-European family all derive from Sanskrit, the language of the ancient Aryans. There are many word similarities between the Sanskrit and Welsh, the few shown below are basic words with usage from early stages of language formation.

English	Welsh	Sanskrit
God	Duw	Adeva
Son	mab	ab
Daughter	Merch(geneth)	agneya
Husband	gwr	agiros
Wife	gwraig	agaryani
Pouring rain	bwrw glaw	bhyriursti
Snow	eira	tusara
Food	bwyd	abhyasta
Wet	gwlyb	klid
Tooth	dant	dantabhaga

Sanskrit also has many words within its lexicon prefixed with ng which in the Welsh language is a mutation when the consonant c is the first letter.

HISTORICAL LINKS

THE HEBREW - WELSH CONNECTION

Language, Cultural and Religious Ties.

In the eighth century, B.C., the Assyrian Empire was at its peak, and its armies threatened the nations on the eastern Mediterranean seaboard, including Israel. A brutal, fearsome people, the Assyrians conquered lands plundering everything of value - even people, exporting their slavery to foreign lands. Wall murals, some of which now bedeck the British Museum in London, depict scenes of the Assyrians' horrible savagery and torture.

Famed archaeologist Sir Austen Henry Layard, rediscovered and unearthed the ancient Assyrian cities, and described the scenes on the wall murals he found as punishments and tortures beyond the human imagination and that the bleeding heads of the slain were tied round the necks of the living who seemed reserved for still more barbarous tortures.

Inhabitants of Palestine in those days were well aware that Assyria would only too soon conduct a similar brutal warfare against the eastern shore of the Mediterranean. Would not large numbers of Israelites migrate westward, by land and sea, to find safety for themselves and their families outside of the Assyrian sphere of influence?

Historical evidence indicates that did indeed happen. More Israelites migrated voluntarily out of Palestine than even the large numbers of those taken away in the Assyrian and Babylonian captivities. As it became clear that invasion and conquest by Assyria was imminent, Hebrews and Phoenicians emigrated westward by the many hundreds of thousands, forming the foundation of European civilization.

Historians have given the Phoenicians most of the credit for this emigration from Palestine to Europe, although the Hebrews were more numerous, and were Divinely promised greatly increased numbers. Perhaps the answer to the confusion is that the Hebrew language is a Phoenician dialect, and the two are virtually identical. But as we will see, a great multitude of the 'Phoenician' speaking early European colonists can be shown to be Hebrew.

PHOENICIAN-CELTIC LINK

In the 18th century, historians discovered exciting proof of Phoenician-Celtic ties. An ancient Roman dramatist, Titus Maccius Plautus (died 184 B.C.) wrote a play, the *'Penulus'* in which he placed then current Phoenician into the speech of one of his characters. In the 18th century, linguists noticed the great similarity between that Phoenician and the early Celtic language. Modern language scholars have confirmed that there is a definite connection between the Celtic and Hebrew.

RELIGIOUS LINK

Since it is true that Hebrews and Phoenicians migrated to Europe in large numbers in ancient times, there must be religious and cultural ties, and in fact, such connections abound. Dr Thomas Moore's, *History of Ireland* relates: *"That most common of all Celtic monuments, the Cromlech, is to be found not only in most parts of Europe, but also in Asia, including Palestine. Not less ancient and general among the Celtic nations, was the circle of upright stones, with either an altar or tall pillar in the centre, and, like its prototype at Gilgal (ancient Israel), serving sometimes as a temple of worship, sometimes as a place of national council or inauguration ... The rough, unhewn stone... used in their circular temples by the Druids, was the true, orthodox observance of the divine command".*

In Europe, Stonehenge, Avebury, and many other early Celtic sites were designed in a circular pattern.

GEOGRAPHICAL LINK

Celtic scholar, Sir John Rhys, gives strong evidences of Hebrew colonization of the British Isles in ancient times. He discusses a region *"just in the vicinity of St David's or Mynyw (Menevia), called in the Welsh Chronicle MONI IUDEORUM, which contains an allusion probably to the same people."* Sir John says that some scholars suggest this word, Iudeorurn or Judeorurn, may relate to the 'Jutes', a Germanic tribe in Northern Europe, but that he believes such a view incorrect. Instead, he indicates that it identifies Hebrews of the tribe of Judah adding, *"... lastly we seem to have a trace of the same form in the Welsh Chronicle, sometimes called Annales Cambriae, when it calls Menevia or St. David's Moni Iudeorum".* He also discusses early Celtic names and suggests that we *"... compare Semitic names ... compare the Hebrew."*

One last fascinating connection with ancient Israel is suggested by Sir John, who says, *'the (Celtic) Kymry were for some time indifferently called Cambria or Cumbria, the Welsh word on which they are based being, as now written, Cymru ... and is pronounced nearly as an Englishman would treat it if spelled Kumry or Kumri.'* . As students of Old Testament history well know, 'Kumri' or'Khumri' was the name of the Israelites in Assyrian texts. The virtual identity in spelling and sound between the Israelite 'Khumri', and the Celtic 'Kymry', is too much of a coincidence to not have a relationship. Taken with the many other data, religious and cultural, the connection between the ancient Hebrews and Celts is too strong to be ignored.

In fact, it is no longer a question of, *"Did Hebrews settle in Europe in ancient times?"* but a question of, *"How many of the people of Europe are of Hebrew descent?"*

SUMMARY

Therefore we can say that in all of these and indeed in a multitude of other ways, the Celts and Hebrews bear a remarkable relationship. Since the Celts were spread over most of Europe, the cultural, historical, and theological implications of this truth are immensely significant.

HEBREW-WELSH CONNECTION

Insular British Celtic tongues, especially colloquial Welsh, says W.H.Worrell, *"show certain peculiarities which are reminiscent of Hamitic and Semitic tongues and are unparalleled in Aryan languages"*.

Certain features (of marginal influence only) of Old Irish verb forms can be understood only in the light of Hittite, Vedic, Sanskrit, and Mycenean Greek. J.Morris Jones said that, *"The pre-Aryan idioms which still live in Welsh and Irish were derived from a language allied to Egyptian tongues"*.

The above linguistic remarks show that Insular Celtic (i.e. of Britain and Ireland as distinct from the Continental forms which were somewhat different) is consistent with the claims proposed herein: i.e. The original tongue of the Insular Celts was Semitic (Hebrew) which marginally was influenced by Mycenean Greek, Hittite, Indo-European (Sanskrit), Syrian, and Mitanni. Heavy Hamitic influences may be attributable to those of some of the neighbouring peoples, such as the Canaanites, and Egyptians, and to having sojourned in a North African environment. In addition, the natives of Spain amongst whom the Insular Celts or a good portion of them once dwelt, traded with, and fought against, were also at least in part of

North African Berber related Hamitic origin. This explanation may sound involved and complicated but it accords with the evidence when archaeological, anthropological, mythological, and linguistic findings are compared with each other. At all events the natives of Wales and Ireland must have used a Hamitic and/or Semitic tongue(s) before they came into contact with Continental Indo-European ones.

HEBREW IN WELSH

It was seen that colloquial Welsh definitely has some type of underlying linguistic base that must derive only from Middle Eastern (Semitic) and/or North African Hamitic sources. This conclusion was derived from the quoted opinions of linguistic scientists still active in their field today. It so happens that in the past there were others who held similar opinions but went further than their present-day counterparts care to, expressing a relationship between Celtic tongues and Hebrew.

In 1832, a writer who signed his name "Glas" submitted a list of Welsh words with Hebrew origins. The writer remarked that, *"But the best proof of the Eastern descent of the ancient British is the close resemblance and connection existing between the Welsh and Hebrew languages, even at this day. As a proof of this we have extracted the following vocabulary of words in both tongues, so closely resembling each other in sound and sense as to leave no doubt whatever on the subject. Many of these words, it will be found, have been transmitted from the Welsh, through the Anglo-Saxon into the modern English. It would be easy to swell their number"*.

Some of the examples adduced by the above writer were:

English	Hebrew	Welsh
he went, he is gone; hence	athah	aeth ef
frequent, plentiful, ample	hamale	aml
the earth	badamah	y byd yma
air, sky	auor	awyr
it came to pass	bo, boten,	bu
paunch, belly	beten	oten
multi-coloured	barud	brith
hatred	caas (anger).	Cas
trickle, or distill by drops	nataph, taph.	dafn(u)

31

Almost two hundred years prior to the above writer, Charles Edwards (*"Hanes y Fydd - 1675"*) published a number of Welsh ambro-Brittanic Hebraisms in which he shows that whole phrases in Welsh can be closely paralleled by whole phrases in Hebrew.

From the list compiled by Charles Edwards, L.G.A. Roberts (1919) made a selection of examples after slightly modernising the Hebrew transliterations. It should be noted that when account is taken for likely and known dialectical changes of pronunciation the examples given in effect show identical Welsh parallel phrases for the Hebrew original.

English	Hebrew	Welsh
Multitude	bagad	bagad, "torf"
Perjure	aen Adon	anudon
I am the Almighty God sy' dda	Ani El Saddai.	Myfi hollalluog
lineage, pedigree	acheinu	achau
Nurse	maynceth	mamaeth
Job answered,	veya(g)nEyub	yngan Job
to increase	umalu	amlhau
heal us	hechiyatni	iachâd ni
sky	aor	awyr
your heads	panechoh	eich penau
next	nasa	nesa
urge, compel	ain ones	annos
nimble, quick	ish chamas	chwimwth
moonlight	leoroe	lloerga
sunny	behilo	heulo
to threaten	biugthi	bygythio
cursed	yu-ar, yuv-ar	ysgeler
reproof	im (c)ge-arato	ceryddu
Tabernacle of Jacob	neoth Yacob	Neuadd Jacob
Praise	galaed	clod

The affinity between Hebrew and Welsh was mentioned by a certain Dr. Davies*, and in the preface to his Welsh Grammar there was a poem to the effect that:

He gladly deigns his countrymen to teach,
By well-weighòd rules, the rudiments of speech;
That when the roots first of our own we gain,
The Hebrew tongue we thence may soon attain .

*The Dr Davies mentioned is probably Dr John Davies of Mallwyd (1567-1644) one of Wales's leading scholars of the late Renaissance.

.

THE DAN TRIBE IN BRITAIN AND EUROPE

The Tribe of the Dan have been traced to Greece, North Africa, and other parts of the ancient and modern world and historian Walter Baucum asks the question, *"Do Danites have any connection to the Celts, who settled in Europe and the British Isles?"* He commenced his research not with people or tribes, but with language, the language of the Celts.

The Irish, Scottish, and Welsh, plus many of the ancient Britons and Gauls, spoke forms of Celtic. Celtic people apparently received the Indo-European aspects of their language and culture from peoples they had conquered on the continent before continuing their westward trek. Linguistic examinations of the speech of the Welsh and Irish reveal a form of Celtic in which there is an underlying speech element similar to that found in North Africa, which languages are classified as "Hamitic". Both Egyptian and Berber are Hamitic tongues.

The work of Yair Davidii in *"Lost Israelite Identity"* concentrates on insular British Celtic tongues, especially colloquial Welsh, showing certain peculiarities which are reminiscent of Hamitic and Semitic tongues and are unparalleled in Aryan languages. Irish has as many features in common with non-Indo-European languages, especially with Hamito-Semitic languages, as with other Indo-European languages. Certain features of Old Irish verb forms can be understood only in the light of Hittite, Vedic, Sanskrit, and Mycenean Greek. The pre-Aryan idioms which still live in Welsh and Irish were derived from a language allied to Egyptian tongues. The conclusion drawn by Davidii is that the original tongue of the Insular Celts was Semitic (Hebrew), which marginally was influenced by Mycenean Greek, Hittite, Indo-European (Sanskrit), Syrian, Mitanni, and some others.

The point that Davidii makes from all this is that both the Irish and the Welsh undoubtedly used a Hamitic and/or Semitic tongue before they came into contact with Continental Indo-European ones. He goes on to state that this is proof that the Celtic peoples of Europe originally spoke Hebrew. It must be understood that the Israelites, in their exile, were divided and scattered and, to a certain degree, had to accept the cultural and linguistic standards of those around them.

The language closest to ancient Hebrew today is Welsh, in many cases identical. Davidii mentions that the Rev. Eliezer Williams (b.1754) wrote several works on the Celts and made several remarks that pertain to this. *"In the Hebrew...which the ancient British language greatly resembles... the roots of most of the ancient British, or real Welsh, words may be regularly traced in the Hebrew...scarcely a Hebrew root can be discovered that has not its corresponding derivative in the ancient British language...but not only...the words...their variations and inflections afford a much stronger proof of affinity... the plural number of nouns likewise is often formed in a similar manner in the Celtic by adding in (a contraction of IM which is the suffix used in Hebrew to form the masculine plural)...in the formation of sentences, and in the government of words...the same syntax might serve for both."*

Dr John Davies in '*Mythology of the Ancient Druids*' asserts that *"Taliesin, the chief Bard, declares that his lore had been detailed in Hebraic...."*

It follows from all the above that though the language of the British Celts may have superficially conformed to an Indo-European type, it had enough Semitic and Hebraic features to confirm the notion that Hebrew had been their original tongue.

We have seen the affiliation of the Dan tribe with Wales, Ireland, Britain, Scandinavia, North Africa, and Greece. But Dan was intermingled also with other Israelite tribes and helped settle West Europe, as well as Scandinavia and Great Britain, as we have seen earlier. These people came to be called Celts and are today the West Europeans, and the significance of a people called Cimmerians.

Exiled Israel was called "Khumri" by their Assyrian captors. They also were called Gimir or Gomer. The term "Gimiri" in Babylon meant "tribes." The similar sounding "gamira" denoted mobility and hints at nomadism, or exile, or both. The Scythians also were called Gimiri, meaning Cimmerian. The Cimmerians first appeared on the fringes of the Assyrian Empire in the Middle East.

In 679 B.C., a group of Cimmerians led by Teushpa was defeated by the Assyrians. A document discovered at Nineveh mentioned "Ubru-Harran, chief of a Cimmerian detachment," serving in the Assyrian forces. The name "Ubru-Harran" is West Semitic and probably Hebrew (Note "Ubru"). The Mesopotamians from Tiglathpileser III on, and later the neo-Babylonian armies, were equipped with "Cimmerian" bows, "Cimmerian" arrows, "Cimmerian" horse harness parts, and even "Cimmerian" footwear.

The Cimmerians first became known, according to Walter Baucum, in what later came to be known as "Iberia" (which also implies "Hebrew"), where legends relate that the Lost Ten Tribes had been taken, and followed them into Europe. It was very soon, almost immediately, that these Cimmerians had first appeared after the Israelites were exiled. Their very name might be a form of "Khumri," which appellation the Assyrians themselves applied to Israel. They were destined to advance into Europe, where they overran the Halstatt civilization.

From the Middle East then, these Cimmerians moved into Europe by way of the Balkans and the Danube Valley. They became an important factor in the formation of the "Celtic" peoples, as were the Cimmerian-related Scyths. Parts of the Cimmerians, the Scyths, and the Goths (both of whom had been part of the Cimmerians originally) gave rise to the Anglo-Saxon, Frank, Scandinavian, and related people.

From about 1200 B.C., the Urnfield Culture had dominated central and western Europe. Urnfield culture preceded Halstatt, its peoples were mixed Orientals and 'Indo-Europeans', and they were to give the Cimmerian dominated iron-using civilisation of Halstatt its European flavour. The early 'Cimmerians' themselves were believed to have been largely of Israelite origin. The centres of Halstatt civilisation for a while were in south Germany and from there apparently emerged the Celtic language in its Indo-European dress. Out of this, we are told, the Halstatt civilization developed. Although in disagreement as to when this change occurred, most historians today generally accept 700 B.C. What caused it? It appears that groups of conquerors from the East identified as Cimmerian, appeared first in Hungary, then westward to the southern parts of the North Alpine province. Bronze horse bits and bridle mounts, closely related in form to types found on the Pontic steppes in Caucasia all the way to Iran, which appears to indicate the presence of the Cimmerian and Israelite "cavalry," which have been found in this area. These horsemen had far-flung connections over the steppes where these Israelite and Cimmerian exiles had been involved. Their contribution was a stimulus in things martial and in improved horse management, and may even have been veteran mercenaries from the armies of Assyria and Urartu.

Cimmerian migrations can be traced from the Assyrian-dominated Middle East across Europe into Britain. They were noted for their equestrian specialties, as the exiled Israelites had been. Piggott says, "*The Cimmerians have been invoked as an ultimate agent in the further adoption of cavalry from the seventh century onwards by the contemporary civilizations of antiquity.*"

The Celts were believed to have come from the east and to have advanced via the Danube Valley. Welsh legend stated that their ancestors the Cymry had been led by Hu Gadarn from Drephane opposite Byzantium (on the Bosporus). Bosporus, also called Cimmerian Bosporus, was an ancient Greek state situated on Kerch Strait in present-day southern Ukraine. Jewish tradition said that part of the Lost Ten Tribes had gone to

Daphne of Antiochia which is identifiable with Drephane whence came the Cymry. This account accords with what is known concerning the Cimmerians and their Celtic offspring who arrived in Europe overland from the same direction and bearing essentially the same name and culture.

Diodorus Siculus linked the Cimmerians of old, the Galatians, and the Cimbri all together. Plutarch (in 'Marius') reported the opinion that the Cimmerians, Cimbri, and Scythians were in effect all members of the one nation whom he calls 'Celto-Scythians.' Homer placed the Cimmerians in the British Isles as did a poem allegedly written c.500 B.C. by the Greek Orpheus.

The ideas expressed by ancient sources correspond with what is known today concerning the historical and archaeological background. The Cimmerians became the Cimbri of the north, the Cymry of Britain and the Galatians and other Celtic entities. There were Israelite tribes amongst them which therefore to a degree must have been identical with them. The Lost Ten Tribes of Israel are to be sought for amongst descendants of the Cimmerii and related peoples who settled in Western Europe.

To summarize, about 650 B.C., Cimmerian Celts appeared in Halstatt areas, invaded Italy, and continued to Spain. They settled in Spain and were later re-enforced by La Tène Celtic elements. In Spain these Cimmerian-Celts amalgamated with the Hiberi (Hebrews), who associated with Tarshish and who influenced their culture. These Hebrews had been transported overseas after the Assyrian conquest of Israel to Spain by Phoenicians in Assyrian employ. In the 500's B.C., the combined Israelite Cimmerians-and-Hiberi (from Spain) were established on the Rhone in southern France. Then North African "Iberians" and Carthaginians drove them out of Spain and northwards from the Rhone. These Celts who emerged from Spain are, roughly speaking, those who identified themselves as Hiberi and who were also known as Galatae. Hiberi derived from the word "Hebrew" and Galatae itself being a form of "Gilead," who was a grandson of Manasseh and founder of an extremely important tribal clan of independent status amongst the Tribes of Israel, according to Yair Davidii.

The work of Yair Davidii continues to provide ancestral evidence with place and people names within Europe in "The Hebrews of Britain,". Of all the names associated with Israel in the Celtic world, perhaps "Eber," meaning "Hebrew," is the most important. We find it spread throughout Europe, especially in Britain. The early Celtic settlers in Britain referred to themselves as "Hiberi" (or "Iberi") and are even named such by Ptolemy himself. They called Ireland Hibernia; there were the Hebrides Islands, plus many places in Gaul and other Celtic areas whose names contained the root "eber." Davidii quotes Bennett *"...there were twenty or more places in Wales, the names of which begin with another form of the name Eber (Aber)"*.

The Israelite peoples called themselves Hebrews, "Hebrew" in the Scriptures being synonymous with Israelite. There were twelve Israelite tribes, and Welsh tradition listed twelve different peoples who invaded Britain, all who can be traced to Hebrew or Israelite names. Yair Davidii goes on to say that representatives of all the tribes settled within the British Isles, but that the dominating elements belonged to the tribes of Joseph (Ephraim and Manasseh). Much of Manasseh emigrated to North America, not forgetting the already mentioned Danites in Ireland and Wales.

What we have is a wealth of evidence suggesting that all of these different groups - Cimmerians, Galatae, Cymry, Cimbri, Helvetti, Belgae, British, Halstatt, Iberi, Iberians, etc. are either the same peoples coming in different waves and re-generating or at the very least, mixed in with other non-Israelite peoples who accepted the customs of the Israelites. That intermarriage took place was inevitable; that much, if not most of this intermarriage was among different Israelite tribes seems almost without doubt.

But what about Wales itself? The flag of Wales depicts a dragon, a symbol of Dan. Green is the national color of Simeon in Rabbinical tradition, and green is the national color of Ireland and, along with white, forms the background of the Welsh flag. Some of Simeon are in Wales, probably. Shaul, one of the sons of Simeon, became the Silures of south Wales. These were a fierce darkish people according to descriptions.

A series of discoveries, revolutionary interpretations and reconstructions of history are bringing us remarkable revelations, asking new questions while at the same time offering new perspectives. Are all the peoples living to the north of the Pyrenees, the Alps, the Carpathian and Caucuses mountains, descendants of the Assyrians and the Ten Lost tribes of Israel?

The eminent Greek historian, Professor Cosmas Megalommitis writes of the scientific approach to the Ten Tribes of Israel that all Assyriologists have believed for some years, that the *Bit Ghumri* (changed to "Gomer" in Biblical Hebrew, and to "Cimmerians," in Greek), as well as the *Ishkuzi* (an Assyrian form of the Urartuan "Ishki Gulu," later changed to "Ashkenazim" in Hebrew and to "Scythians," in Greek), came from Central Asia and, having crossed the Caucuses, settled in the outskirts of North-East Assyria.

Hence, the *Bit Ghumri* are in fact the Ten Tribes of Israel, transported to Zagros, to whom many Assyrian texts refer, describing their activity in Zagros (as well as their arrival in that mountainous region).

Megalommitis continues, saying the trail of the Scythians and Cimmerians, who had become completely intermingled by 650 B.C., has long been known: first northward up to the Caucuses, and then, after crossing this mountainous area, to the north-west and west, across the Ukrainian plains, parallelling the north coast of the Black Sea. Thus they spread into an almost deserted northern Europe, right to its north-west extremities, from where they crossed into the British Isles. *Cimbrians*, *Celts* and *Teutons* all make up the ancient substrate common to all the peoples and races of northern Europe, from Russia to the British Isles.

CULTURES

Bell-Beaker culture

The earliest recorded evidence of man in northern Britain dates to c. 8500 B.C. Neolithic tribes from Spain and France had already made their way to northern Britain. Some archaeologists suggest that these people may have built and used the great chambered cairns which dot what is now the Scottish countryside. It has also been suggested that their descendants eventually merged with the Beaker people (who probably came from northern Europe), and this ethnic union made up the pre-Celtic stock of northern Britain. These became the Brythonic tribe.

The link of these early inhabitants to their Iberian ancestors can be found in the many spiral pattern grooves cut into the rocks and boulders of this northern land and which can also be found in Spain, France and Ireland. The design of burial chambers located in the Orkney islands also provide an important link to the Iberian origin of their builders.

In the late Neolithic era and early Bronze Age, at least two groups of people migrated to Britain, one from northern Europe and the other from Spain and Portugal. People of both groups buried their dead singly under round mounds of earth called round barrows. This type of burial was evident in Wales at that time, and in these graves archaeologists have found distinctive-looking drinking cups, or beakers, thus these people have come to be known as the Beaker folk, or Beaker people. There is also evidence that burial rites changed under the Beaker culture to standing stones - *meini hirion.*

The Beaker folk brought copper technology to Wales and the rest of Britain. They also introduced better farming methods, including the cultivation of barley, improving cattle stocks whilst it is believed that they may also have introduced an Indo-European language.

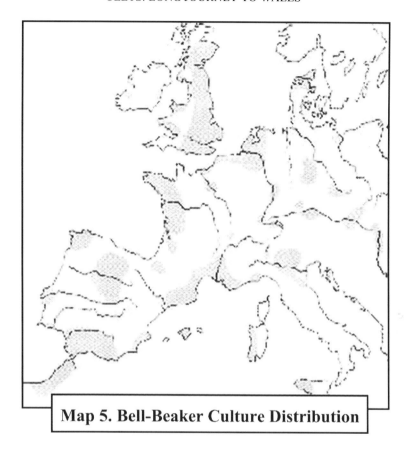

Map 5. Bell-Beaker Culture Distribution

Corded-Ware Culture

Two influencing means of establishing migrational links are the Corded-Ware and Bell-Beaker cultures. The wide-spread Corded Ware culture complex (c. 2900 - 2400 B.C.) derives its name from the frequent use of decorative cord impressions on the clay and ceramic pots etc. The pottery roughly covers the former territory of the Funnel Beaker and related cultures. Some have argued that the Corded Ware represents another invasion from the eastern steppe region, perhaps indicating the introduction of the Indo-European language group.

In the east Corded Ware Culture reached Tatarstan just north of the Pontic steppes in northern Turkey linking this to the ancient Iranian-speaking tribe the Cimmerians, adding potency to the supposition that this tribe were the ancestors of the peoples of North Wales. Ancient-Greek authors defined hordes of horseback nomadic tribes which were called Cimmerians (Iranian-speakers), who highlighted the plight of Asiatic

41

nomads in Europe. At that time Central Asia was beginning to suffer food shortages for both its human population and its cattle due to the rise in global temperature, consequently masses of peoples from Asia began their gradual expansion both west and eastwards where they could pillage or settle.

Excavation evidence provides links with Corded Ware culture, even at a linguistic level, supporting the presence of Indoeuropean languages, thus strongly suggesting a near to middle eastern origin for this culture, further suggesting that at some transmigrational point, the Cimmerians contributed to this culture. Shells from the Red Sea have been found in various parts of Europe in Corded Ware pottery.

Types of vessels include beakers, and often very wide amphorae. The pottery is usually brown to a tan ochre color. Some pottery is impressed with round or even rectilinear holes and cord impressions are common. Necks are frequently decorated and often elongated. Similarly, the upper belly of the amphoras are often heavily decorated.

In many countries it is assumed that the economy was primarily based on cattle. A semi-nomadic or transhumant herding is often envisioned. However, more recently it has become clear that land use depends on the region. While there are overall similarities in pottery and axe style, the local economies were tailored to their individual environments. Again this is consistent with the culture of the Cimmerians.

Hallstatt Culture

An interesting feature of the Hallstatt culture is that it is named after a village in Austria situated by a lake in the region known as Salzkamergut, whose capital is Salzburg. Salzkamergut means *'the place of good salt'*, indicating the importance of salt to the area. It is thought that salt has been mined at Hallstatt for over two and a half thousand years, and that some of the early salt-miners were most certainly Celt—the word *'hall'* is Celtic for salt; the word *'hallt'* is Welsh for salty and *'halen'* is the Welsh for salt.

The term Hallstatt now refers generally to Late Bronze and Early Iron Age culture in central and western Europe. During excavation between 1846 and 1899, more than 2,000 graves were found at Hallstatt. Because of the preservative nature of the salt, implements, parts of clothing, and even the bodies of the miners themselves have been discovered. The majority of the human remains fall into two groups, an earlier (c. 1100/1000 to c. 800/700 BC) and a later (c. 800/700 to 450 BC).

Hallstatt remains are generally divided into four phases (A, B, C, and D), although there is some disagreement among scholars as to how these phases should be dated. In Phase A iron was rare. Cremation was practiced in cemeteries of flat graves (or under very low mounds).

Phase B, confined to the western regions, was marked by the reassertion of the Old Bronze Age population of southwest Germany over the comparatively new Urnfield peoples. The tumulus (barrow) again became common in burial, and cremation is predominant. The pottery (sometimes polychrome) is extremely well made.

In Phase C iron came into general use. Both cremation and inhumation (interment) were used, and the pottery was both polychrome and unpainted. Among the many metal types were: long, heavy iron and bronze swords with scrolled chapes (the metal mounting at the upper end); the winged Hallstatt axe; and long, bronze girdle mounts.

Phase D is not represented in the area around eastern Austria, but it lasted until the appearance of the La Tène (q.v.) period in other areas. The burial rite was mostly inhumation; the pottery, which is not common, degenerates in style and technique. Among the metal objects represented were: the dagger sword with "horseshoe" or antennae hilt; a variety of brooches and ring ornaments; and girdle mounts, sometimes in pierced work. Early archaic Greek vessels appear in the west.

Hallstatt art in general is severely geometric in style; the advances made were on technical rather than aesthetic lines.

La Tène culture

The picture is at best an exciting though an indeterminate one. Nothing can ever be considered to be wholly conclusive, the chronicles and images presented being far too complex to form any clear picture of the Indo-European expansion. But the evidence supplied suggesting our tribal ancestors were the Cimmerians who in turn became part of the vast nation of Celts, arriving in the ancient northern part of Britain and eventually migrating to Edeyrnion, gives valid support to this theory.

The culture offering anything which is remotely near to providing conclusive proof of our ancestral link is that provided by a late Bronze Age culture which existed in central and western Europe known from their typical burial rites as the 'Urnfields'. The succeeding culture is classified by archaeologist's as La Tène. This has been seen as existing from at least as early as the sixth century B.C. continuing until the Roman conquest. During the La Tène phase, Celts were found as widespread as Turkey and the north of Britain, attesting further the link between the Celts of Wales and many tribes of eastern origin.

La Tène, artefacts of which have been discovered in the far north of Britain, is so named after the ancient Celtic site discovered on Lake Neûchatel, Switzerland. Though the culture itself is not indigenous to that part of the world, it does nevertheless give its name to the second and final period of the European Iron Age. It is characterized by an art style that drew upon Greek, Etruscan, and Scythian/Cimmerian motifs, transferring them into highly abstract designs in metal, pottery, and wood. The earliest phase of Tènian culture, from the 6th to the late 5th cent. B.C., spread from the middle Rhine region eastwards into the Danube valley, south into Switzerland, and Westwards and Northwards into France, the Low Countries, Denmark, and the British Isles. Tenian culture flourished until subjected to the advances of the Roman Empire. The Celtic peoples of the La Tène period borrowed much from older civilizations, including the Etruscan chariot, woodworking tools that enabled them to clear temperate forests for planting, and Greek agricultural implements such as the rotary millstone. The Indo-European migration was the likeliest conduit for this cultural movement.

The arrival of the Cimmerians on these shores coincides with the introduction of iron in the 7th century B.C. and for three centuries a succession of small migrations ensued, the newcomers apparently assimilating into the ways of existing inhabitants in addition to supplementing the native culture with parts of their own. The earliest ironsmiths made daggers of the Hallstatt type but of a distinctively British form. The settlements were also of a distinctively British type, with the traditional round house, the "Celtic" system of farming with its small fields, and storage pits for grain. Thus ancient Britain absorbed the newcomers.

From the 6th century B.C. swords were making a reappearance in place of daggers culminating in a British form of La Tène Celtic art, developing a decoration of warlike equipment such as scabbards, shields, and helmets, and eventually also bronze mirrors and even domestic pottery.

Another feature linking Wales with the work of these artists is the appearance of dragons on numerous artefacts displaying a pattern in the form of the art introduced by the Cimmerians which was also Scythian in form, many of which are synonymous with Celtic art. There are several characteristics of this Cimmerian art that make it unique from other art styles. Some of these can be found in the arts of other cultures:- a profusion of animals used in one piece or device. The animals are primarily used in a decorative fashion as opposed to a narrative fashion.

Lively depiction of animals, much movement expressed as opposed to the stiff, formal form used in the art of adjacent Near Eastern cultures. "Zoomorphic Juncture" - animals combined with parts of other animals or animals depicted within other animals; circular manifestation of animal shapes or several identical animals in circular formation; distortion or contortion of animal to fit a preconceived shape of ornament such as a rectangle or circle. Animals with head facing backwards over shoulder (inverted) often in reverse pairs; head to head pairs of animals; crouching lioness or cat, nose to the ground. Decorative circular swirls, crescents or oval forms drawn on the haunches of animals indicating muscles. "Flying Leap" posture of deer or cats as well as the frequent addition of bird's heads (known as beak heads) to extremities of animal form together with queued or stacked animals. Another feature of the Sword Style artists is that dragons appear on numerous artefacts, especially weaponry.

Many Pictish stone carvings are to be found in Scotland in what was the ancient Britain, combining several of the patterns as those imported with the Cimmerians, e.g. decorative circular swirls; bird's heads; animals head to head as well as in reversed pairs together with zoomorphic forms. These add further strength to the links between the nomadic Cimmerian tribes of Mesopotamia, Iran and the Russian Steppes and the eventual inhabitants of Edeyrnion.

Pit Grave Culture

From the end of the third through to the first millennium B.C., speakers of ancient European languages spread gradually into Europe. Their coming is demonstrated archaeologically by the arrival of the semi nomadic "pit grave" culture, which buried its dead in shafts, or barrows. A nobleman would be buried with his ceremonial dagger engraved on the shaft (see section on Owain Glyndwr and shaft in Corwen churchyard with the engraving of a dagger) together with precious gems and other decorations placed within the shaft.

The Cimmerians, at one stage of their transmigration, together with the Pit Grave Culture, were located in the southern Steppe area (Ukraine) and it was from the Pit Grave culture in this region c.3000 B.C. the Corded Ware culture spread over Europe.

The long chambered grave, a variant of the collective tomb burials that spread into western and north western Europe from the Aegean area during the final stage of the northern Stone Age (c. 2000 BC) examples of which are segmented graves with concave forecourts found in the southwestern area of Scotland, the home of the ancient Welsh Brythonic tribe.

A new pottery appeared on the mainland: a class of gray burnished ware, wheel-made, with sharp angular shapes copied from those of metal vases. The polished gray surfaces of this "Minyan" ware looked as if it was meant to imitate silver. This appears to be the black/gray coloured pottery attributed to the east-west migrating Cimmerians.

The once-common group burials of the north of ancient Britain were replaced by the individual interments common of the Bronze Age by 2000 B.C. coinciding with the arrival of the Bell Beaker culture, the dead were buried within their cists, but gradually the practice of cremation appears to have found favour, the cremated remains then placed within the burial cist. The cremation and the burial of ashes in urns originated in the southern Netherlands and Belgium (Hilversum culture) arriving in Britain certainly before 700 B.C. And this may well have coincided with the arrival of the Cimmerians whose transmigration would most certainly have passed through this region.

ARCHAEOLOGICAL ANALYSES

DNA, Oxygen and Strontium Isotope Analyses

There appears to be a strong consensus between the various factions of archaeologists, geneticists and historians that there is no doubting that the Indo-European migration did take place. The scale of such a trek is impossible to calculate even with all the modern technology at our disposal. That said however, there is much research that has been undertaken over the years using the techniques of Strontium Isotope Analysis, Oxygen Isotope Analysis and, possibly the more well-known even if a mere infant by comparison, is that of the advance of DNA analysis.

Human skeletal remains from Bell Beaker graves in southern Germany, Austria, the Czech Republic, and Hungary were analysed for information on human migration. Strontium isotope ratios were measured in bone and tooth enamel to determine if these individuals had changed 'geological' residence during their lifetimes. Strontium isotopes vary among different types of rock. They enter the body through diet and are deposited in the skeleton. Tooth enamel forms during early childhood and does not change. Bone changes continually through life. The difference in the strontium isotope ratio between bone and enamel in the same individual indicates a change in regional residence. Results from the analysis of 81 Bell Beaker individuals indicated that 51 had moved during their lifetime, a percentage of 63%.

The information on human movement in ancient times is scant and oxygen isotope analysis of a fair sample of human remains need to enlighten us further. Oxygen has three forms/isotopes, which have different physical properties due to a slight variation in their weights. The oxygen absorbed into the teeth comes mostly from the water that we drink while the teeth are forming. Our drinking water from rain and snow has oxygen isotopes which vary with latitude, altitude, distance from the sea and temperature. By analysing the oxygen in a person's teeth it can be established the kind of climate in which they lived while young and to compare the oxygen values with oxygen isotope maps, thereby establishing where that person was brought up. To date the only reasonable work with such a sample was undertaken in Bavaria where 17 out of 69 individuals sampled were found to have originated elsewhere, a percentage of 25%.

There are two main schools of thought contributing to the debates about human origins; (i) the 'multi-regional evolutionists' believe that *'Homo Ergaster'* spread out of Africa a million plus years ago and in the process colonising much of Eurasia and the Far East, gradually evolving into the modern human *'Homo Sapiens Sapiens'*; (ii) the other camp often termed the *'Garden of Eden'* faction, propose that *'Homo Sapiens Sapiens'* is a new species evolving from *'Homo Ergaster'* separately about a 100,000 years ago and entirely out of Africa.

The biological evidence strongly supports *a 'Garden of Eden'/'Out of Africa'* theory insofar as archaeological excavations have revealed that the earliest modern human skeletons appear in Africa first and in areas of close proximity including parts of the middle-east. Numerous new hominid finds, new absolute datings, and a radical revision of the archaeochronological framework have increasingly placed Africa at the focal point of both Homo sapiens evolution and the origin of modern humans. This is corroborated by recent research on DNA supporting the theory that modern humans evolved in Africa as humans have been there longest.

Archaeologist Colin Renfrew supported the theory that Near-Eastern farmers had technologically, culturally and genetically migrated across Europe. His supposition was that the original proto-Indo-European language came from Asia with the first farmers, and that this dominant culture brought with it a new language and probably new religious ideas, ideals and a new dominant world view.

This theory came under fire from J.P. Mallory who suggested that if Indo-Europeans existed in the eighth millennium B.C., why did its subsequent offshoot languages contain common words for social hierarchies and technologies such as metalworking which he proposes did not exist at the time the original language supposedly spread. This suggestion could itself be countered with the theory of language integration by two (or more) tribes/groups of different origins attempting to communicate with each other at which time language becomes an immediate obstacle. In time these groups successfully develop a new word list comprising existing vocabulary together with a sub-set of entirely new words.

Accepting that the timescale of the original languages of the tribes/groups may be centuries apart, then it is feasible to accept that the resulting hybrid language would include a word list from the more modern of the two which could have introduced some of the common words for social hierarchies and technologies such as metalworking which J.P. Mallory contested did not exist at the time the original language was supposed to have spread.

Undoubtedly the greatest advancement in molecular archaeology is that of DNA analysis which came to the forefront in the 1990's (although DNA was first discovered in 1869, its role in genetic inheritance was not demonstrated until 1943), its acid organic chemical of complex molecular structure which is found in bacterial cells and in many viruses, its codes allowing genetic information for the transmission of inherited traits.

One of the most important research on DNA was carried out by a team of historical geneticists led by Bryan Sykes of Oxford University. This team analysed over eight hundred samples across Europe, identifying seven major clusters into which fit 95% of modern native Europeans. These clusters varied in age between 45,000 and 10,000 years, suggesting that European origins are far more complex than what is indicated by the Eastern migrating-farmers model. Only one in seven clusters seemed to originate among the pioneering farmers of Asia, a percentage of over 14%, but nevertheless, an adequate percentage to provide evidence of movement from the ancient east to the west.

What is significant here is that the clusters analysed were well outside of the Indo-European chronology and would have no bearing on the Eastern migrants model, therefore casting some doubt on such results. The reason for this is that it must be borne in mind that the Indo-European migration may well have commenced within Europe (many scholars are convinced that this was within the Russian Steppe area), travelling eastwards before once again journeying westwards. This theory would comply with DNA analysis of the Indo-European conforming with that of the modern European. It must be understood that the Indo-European expansion was not a continuous trek, that tribes/nations would establish colonies extending for lengthy periods of time before a new journey would commence.

Many academics have expressed the opinion that molecular archaeology and DNA studies parallel a runaway steam train; sparks fly in all directions and has difficulty staying on the rails. We also need to question the possibility of the risks involved in the contamination of material taken from burial sites. This process involves the grounding of bones taken from these sites back to laboratories thus making cross-contamination a possibility. It remains that new techniques, whilst appearing impressive, may still generate erroneous results inviting greater caution to be exercised. The work carried out by various archaeologist's using oxygen and strontium isotope analysis cannot be lightly dismissed as this has conclusively recognised the movement of prehistoric human migration.

A major flaw in the final analyses in the work of Bryan Sykes I believe is that whilst DNA analysis on skeletal human remains offers more precision in its scientific analyses than any other form, no data would be available from the remains of the ashes of the dead following cremation. The absence of such data present difficulties and makes any final analyses erroneous, therefore it cannot be ruled out that the percentage of Eastern migrating-farmers was greater than 14%, and now Bryan Sykes believes this figure to be nearer 20% whilst Cavill Sforza's work suggests this is nearer 25%. A recent study of Y chromosone haplotypes from modern Europeans favours the demic diffusion model, proposing that 50% of the gene's contribution came from immigrant farmers.

Various sources cite the practice of cremation on open fires being introduced to the Western world by the Greeks as early as 1000 BC. who adopted this from more northern tribes as an imperative of war and nomadism.

There is no mention as to the source of the northern tribes but this could well have been any one or a number of the Indo-European tribes during their transmigration which most certainly would have been *'in transit'* during the period 1000 B.C. and most certainly to the north of Greece. The origin of cremation in Europe was in the period between 2000 B.C - 700 B.C. in the southern region of the Netherlands and Belgium.

It is indeed possible that the practice of cremation was adopted fom India during the Indo-European transmigration as at one time a fragment invaded the Indus Valley civilization where the custom of cremation is ancient and regarded very desirable by Hindus. And so it is possible that a similar tribute was practised for those nomads whose lives ended during the transmigration.

We must accept that the majority of DNA analysis would favour the static indigenous population and that the revised figures of 20% from Bryan Sykes's and 25% from Cavill Sforza's research respectively still represents a large enough proportion supporting the Eastern migrating-farmers model that the Indo-European transmigration did take place. Indeed, DNA analysis in various sites within France and Germany by the same geneticist confirmed that there was a gene flow linked with the spread of farming to Europe from Middle-Eastern populations. Further evidence of the unmistakable east-west diffusion is given in the conclusion from the research of Y chromosones carried out in 1997 by Ornella Simeno.

Finally, there is a clear danger with DNA results that observed differences may be associated with known historical events when many alternative explanations could explain these. What is interesting however is that a group of researchers at the University College, London, examined DNA samples from the modern population within Wales and England and observed a clear difference between these. The main conclusion arrived at was that the Welsh are the true natives of the British Isles whilst the English were *'recent newcomers'* bearing a similarity to the people of Frisia (a historic region of the Netherlands and Germany fronting the North Sea which includes the Frisian Islands).

Is it therefore not time that the Welsh nation was recognised as the true parent-Celt of the British Isles?

THE BRYTHONIC

Following a time span of some 2,500 years and having travelled a distance of approximately 12,000 miles, the great Indo-European expansion had arrived in ancient Britain, its subsequent melting pot giving birth to the Brythoniaid / Brythonic and Votadini tribes, who ultimately became the people of Edeyrnion.

It was a Greek geographer, Pytheas of Massilia, who, navigating the western sea-route 325-323 BC, described the British Isles as Pretanic. This ancient name for Britain survives today in the Welsh word for Britain - Prydain. It is, according to the late Professor Gwyn A. Williams, a genuine Celtic word deriving from a form of speech which became Brittonic, the language of the island of Britain.

The indigenous linguistic history of the north of ancient Britain presents us with a changing tapestry of cultures throughout the recorded history of the last two millennia. Broadly speaking, the two regions in question are the north of the river Forth, specifically the modern county of Fife, and the south of the river, mainly the modern region of Lothian, with its three modern counties plus that of Edinburgh. For much of that time, it is the Celtic languages of Brythonic (Old Welsh), Pictish, and Scottish Gaelic (Gàidhlig) which dominate these two regions, but the Germanic languages of Anglian (Northern Anglo-Saxon) and Scots also successively figure in their history.

What we now call the "Celtic" group of languages were first properly classified as such by the Scottish theorist, George Buchanan (1506-1582), himself a Gaelic speaker and renowned Latin scholar. Indeed, some of the more sceptical of today's scholars claim that Buchanan more-or-less fabricated the entire concept of the Celts in the first place. But since Buchanan first noted the similarities between the languages we now classify as "Celtic", two primary branches have been distinguished by modern linguists: the Brythonic and Goidelic branches. In modern terms, the Brythonic languages include Welsh (Cymraeg), Cornish (Kernewek), and Bréton (Brezhoneg). The Goidelic languages include Irish (Gaeilge), Scottish Gaelic (Gàidhlig), and Manx (Gaelg).

A similar classification to describe this split in the Celtic family of languages into two branches denotes the Goidelic branch as "q-Celtic" and the Brythonic branch as "p-Celtic". Basically, this refers to the way in which the hard "k" sounds in Goidelic languages seems to have transformed in time into the soft "p" sounds of the Brythonic languages (it is generally assumed that the q-Celtic branch is older than the p-Celtic branch). Hence, the Gaelic word for "son of" is mac, whereas the Welsh word is ap. Equally, the Gaelic for "head" is ceann, whereas the Welsh is pen. The classification of q-Celtic and p-Celtic languages were first introduced in the nineteenth century, but is still commonly used by linguists and historians to this day. In ancient history, the majority of Britain is often claimed to have spoken forms of p-Celtic or Brythonic (known in its later manifestations as Old Welsh), although the Picts of north-eastern Scotland appear to have spoken a variant of Brythonic which still eludes precise classification due to the lack of substantial literary remains in that language.

This combination of Gaelic and Pictish cultures may go some way to explaining some of the differences between the Irish and Scottish forms of Gaelic - for example, common northern Scottish placename elements such as strath (eg. Strathspey) and aber (eg. Aberdeen) are Brythonic, not Goidelic. In northern cases, such elements are specifically Pictish, but both words are still current in modern Welsh as strad and aber. These place name elements are rare in Ireland, the historical heartland of the modern Goidelic languages. In many senses, the early historical languages of Southern Scotland present a simpler case, being easily identifiable as Brythonic, the forerunner of modern Welsh. Indeed, the first poem to survive in Old Welsh *(Hwn yw y Gododdin)* was actually written in Lothian by the poet Aneirin around 600 AD.

It should also be noted, however, that Scots, one of the major modern Scottish languages, is not in fact a Celtic language, but Germanic, being a close relative of English, deriving from Northern Anglo-Saxon (ie. Anglian) with seventh century roots in the Lothians. But that, as they say, is another story, and the primary cultures which influenced the place names which Inchcolm has had involve specifically Celtic, rather than Germanic aspects.

Overall, then, the shifting pattern of languages in the regions of ancient Britain break down as follows: a Brythonic or Old Welsh-speaking culture South of the River Forth in Lothian, which changes to the Germanic languages of Anglian and then Scots from around the seventh century, by which time the Old Welsh had *'migrated'* to North Wales along with Cunedda and the Votadini tribe. North of the Forth, in Fife, we find a Pictish culture with its apparent Brythonic associations gradually being transformed into a Gaelic-speaking culture, possibly around the end of the first millennium, with Scots slowly making inroads into the region after the thirteenth century.

According to Christopher Hawkes (1973) the modern Brythonic languages all derive from a common ancestral language termed *Common Brythonic*, *Old Brythonic* or *Proto-Brythonic*, which is thought to have developed from the Proto-Celtic language which was introduced to Britain from the middle-second millennium B.C.. Brythonic languages were then spoken at least in the whole of Great Britain south of the rivers Forth and Clyde, presumably also including the Isle of Man. The theory has been advanced (notably by R. F. O'Rahilly) that Ireland was populated by speakers of Brythonic before being displaced by speakers of a Q-Celtic language (possibly from the Quarietii tribe of southern France, although the linguists Dillon and Chadwick reject this theory as being implausible.

During the period of the Roman occupation of Britain (AD 43 to c. 425), common Brythonic borrowed a large stock of Latin words, both for concepts unfamiliar in the pre-urban society of Celtic Britain such as tactics of warfare and urbanisation and rather more mundane words which displaced native terms (most notably, the word for "fish" in all the Brythonic languages derives from the Latin *piscus* rather than the native *'iskos'*). Approximately eight hundred of these Latin loan-words have survived in the three modern Brythonic languages.

It is probable that during this period common Brythonic was differentiated into at least two major dialect groups- Southwestern and Western (in addition we may posit additional dialects spoken in what is now England which have left little or no evidence). Between the end of the Roman occupation and the mid sixth century the two dialects began to diverge into recognisably separate languages, the Western into Cumbric and Welsh and the Southwestern into Cornish and its closely related sister language Breton, which was carried from the south of Britain to continental Armorica by refugees fleeing the Saxon invaders.

The Brythonic languages spoken in Scotland, the Isle of Man and England were displaced at the same time by Goidelic and Old English speaking invaders.

THE VOTADINI

There is a dearth of information on the Votadini which is quite disappointing considering their chronology was later than the Agathyrsai, Picts, Scythian and Cimmerians. That said, it would appear the Votadini were the amalgam of the settlers of this great migration of the Indo-European together with the indigenous Brythonic peoples.

In *"The Welsh Lineage of John Lewis"*, Grace Moses writes that "the Votadini were a tribe descended from the migrations of Celts from the Caucasus area in Asia, crossing Europe and finally settling the British Isles". The Goutodin kingdom was probably created out of Coel Hen's kingdom of Northern Britain. It is probable that Votadini was the Latin name conferred by the Romans upon the Gododdin/Goutodin, and that they had descended from the indigenous tribe (the Brythonic) and those tribes including the Cimmerians which had migrated to northern Britain.

Possibly long before the Roman's came to these shores the Votadini tribe of Celts had been formed but were known as the Gododdin, occupying the eastern half of the ancient British kingdom of the north which included the modern-day south of Scotland and north of England. The name is a Latin version of the Brythonic form Goutodin or Gododdin which refers to both the people and to the region. Their territory lay south of the Firth of the Forth and extended from the Stirling area down to the River Tyne including at its peak of what are now the Lothian and Borders regions of eastern Scotland, and Northumberland in north-east England. The boundaries with other tribes are uncertain, and those living around Stirling were known as the *Manaw (Manau) Gododdin*.

The Manaw Gododdin were a subsidiary of the main Gododdin people who lay just beyond the Antonine Wall, around the Forth's headwaters and a natural citadel at Stirling. It is from here that Cunedda Wledig, founder of Gwynedd migrated to North Wales. The Anglo-Saxon Bernician historian Bede mentions Stirling as *"urbs Guidi"*, and this was adapted to provide the Firth of Forth with its early Welsh name of *merin Iodeo, 'the sea of Iudeu'*.

Centered on its capital of Din Eidyn and later called Edinburgh by the Angles people were probably living in the region of Edinburgh about 1500 B.C. The name Edinburgh derives from Dineidin, mentioned in Y Gododdin by Aneirin. Din or dun is Celtic for fort. Eidin or Edin is the ancient name for hill. The Saxon for dun is burgh.

The kingdom could also call upon Traprain Law (Haddington in

Lothian) to act as a substitute capital (this perhaps pre-dating Din Eidyn). The later name of Lothian has its base in Goutodin (later Gododdin), which itself is a British version of Votadini. Din Eidyn itself may have been a separate, or sub-kingdom for a time during the 7th century. The border of Goutodin extended less far south than the Votadini lands, probably terminating at Berwick, a scene of later conflict with the Bernician Angles. This region, between Hadrian's and the Antonine Walls, was under direct Roman military rule between AD 138-162, and after that was organised as a buffer state, reaping many of the rewards of alliance with Rome, but not under its rule.

Following the Roman invasion of Britain, including everything south of Hadrian's wall, the Votadini tribe was one of the most northern tribes to fall under the Romans. In addition to their existing Celtic names, Latin versions were ascribed to the Votadinis. The first of these was Tegid ap Cein (Tacitus) born c.270 AD, his son Padarn ap Tegid (Paternus), born c.305 AD, and grandson Edern ap Padarn (Aeternus), born c.364 AD, were all rulers of the Votadini tribe. Edern's son Cunedda Wledig, born c.380 AD, ruled a peaceful and very prosperous tribe who maintained their fighting edge. During this time, the Irish (Professor Gwyn A. Williams refers to these Irish invaders as the Feni, so possibly these were the Cotofeni, originally from the Danube area of Roumania) were invading and settling areas of North Wales of which the ruling Vortigern (Wyrtgeorn 425–450) the over king of Wales, decided to make an offer to Cunedda. This offer was that Cunedda could have most of the land of North Wales if he succeeded in driving the Irish out. As the region was largely uninhabited by the Welsh, Vortigern saw this as a golden opportunity to provide a buffer zone between southern Wales, an unpopulated and largely wilderness area of the north, and populate it with a formidable ally, namely the Votadini. Cunedda drove the Irish from the region and moved many of his tribe to what was to become his kingdom of Gwynedd. Cunedda married the daughter of Coel Hen (of Old King Cole fame), high king of North Britain, over-king of many of the northern tribes of ancient Britain. Some dispute has occurred over time as to whether Cunedda was requested for this campaign by Vortigern or Maximus Wledig which is easily settled by the fact that Vortigern was thriving up to 450 A.D. whilst Maximus Wledig had perished in 388.

The Goutodin kingdom was probably created out of Coel Hen's kingdom of Northern Britain, as there are no rulers listed until after his powerful reign. It was his death which began the gradual division of the north, and the Southern Goutodin territory of Bernaccia became independent at this time. Goutodin quickly fragmented under pressure from the later Bernician Angles.

The area was settled as early as 3000 B.C. and offerings of that period imported from Cumbria and Wales left on the sacred hilltop at Cairnpapple Hill, West Lothian, show that by this time there was a link with these areas. By around 1500 B.C. Traprain Law, East Lothian, was already a place of burial, with evidence of occupation and signs of ramparts after 1000 B.C.

Brythonic Celtic culture and language spread into the area at some time after the 8th century B.C., possibly through cultural contact rather than mass invasion, and systems of kingdoms developed. Numerous hillforts and settlements support the image of quarrelsome tribes and petty kingdoms recorded by the Romans, though evidence that at times occupants neglected the defences might suggest that symbolic power was sometimes as significant as warfare.

In the 1st century the Romans recorded the Votadini as a British tribe. Since the 3rd century Roman Britain had been divided into provinces, and in the last reorganisation a fifth province called Valentia was created, which included the Votadini territory. In the wake of Roman withdrawal around 400 A.D. *Coel Hen* (Old King Cole), who Kessler suggests may have been the last of the Roman *Duces Brittanniarum* (Dukes of the Britons), took over the northern capital at *Eburacum* (York) and became High King of Northern Britain ruling over what had been the northern provinces. After his death the North began to divide, and by about 470 A.D. most Votadini lands became the separate kingdom of Gododdin, while the southern Votadini territory between the rivers Tweed and Tyne formed its own separate kingdom called Brynaich.

THE CELTS

The difficulties in establishing a precise lineage determining our ancient past is rightly seen to be both a linguistic and an archaeological problem. Drawing together the myriad strands and connecting these to the theory of the Indo-European expansion, it is almost certain that the first persons to reach Europe, and eventually the British Isles, speaking an early Indo-European language were the first farmers who came out of western Asia.

Tracing the Celtic settlement of the British Isles proves difficult in that it appears there are two extremes to choose between. The Bell-Beaker culture arrived about 2000 B.C. and according to Gwyn A. Williams, was the period during which the fundamental human society took shape in ancient Britain. Then from 550 B.C. the Early Iron Age people who constructed the hill-forts so characteristic of the insular Celtic world appeared on these islands.

The nearest we get to being precise is that the Celts we have descended from were an amalgam of the Bronze Age Tumulus Culture (1550 - 1250 BC) and those of the Urnfield Culture (1300 BC).

The development of the full European Bronze Age is seen as representing a continuity with the preceding Bell-Beaker phase, but that during the later stages of the Bronze Age a new burial custom, that of cremation, is seen over much of central Europe. It was generally recognized that the Hallstatt culture, which preceded La Tène, was represented by Celtic-speaking peoples. This poses the question as to whether its late bronze age predecessor, the Urnfield culture, was responsible in bringing the first Celtic speakers to western Europe and the British Isles, or whether much earlier cultures such as the Corded Ware Culture became the Proto-Brythonic group.

Following on from the Indo-European expansion, the Celts became a group of peoples that occupied lands stretching from the British Isles to Galatia (the peninsula of land that today constitutes the Asian portion of Turkey). The Celts had many dealings with other cultures that bordered the lands occupied by these peoples, and even though there is no written record of the Celts we can piece together a fair picture of them from archaeological evidence as well as historical accounts from other cultures.

THE ROMANS

The Roman Emperor Claudius ordered the conquest of Britain in A.D. 43., the invasion itself being launched on 22nd March of that year, when an armada of a thousand galleys and transports set off across the Channel from the port of Gesoriacum (Boulogne) on the coast of Gaul. The fleet, a massive army by ancient standards, carried no less than 40,000 troops.

It was a letter written by the wife of a Roman officer, discovered in a soggy patch of ground which gave light to a Britain emerging from prehistory. This was made at the fort of Vindolanda, the site of a Roman garrison in the north of Britain, which housed the garrison's redundant archives in the period prior to the building of Hadrian's Wall. Most of the letters were written in ink on thin wooden tablets the size of modern postcards, the ink being a mixture of carbon, water and gum arabic, with limewood being the most common type of wood used for the tablets, these being easily folded together to protect the inner surface.

Among the documents there are, surprisingly, no accounts of battles or skirmishes of any kind with local tribesmen. One memorandum refers disparagingly to the 'Brittunculi' translated as 'the little Brits' or 'wretched Britons'. These papers, named the 'Vindolanda documents', so named after the ancient military fort, revealed much concerning administrative arrangements and practical needs of the garrison and its relationship with the Roman network in northern Britain. It is not surprising to discover that those who made up the garrison were not Roman, or even Italian by birth. Most of the troops were Batavians or Tungrians from the Low Countries.

By A.D. 61, the Romans controlled the country as far north as the Humber and as far west as the Severn. They had subdued the British tribes up to Yorkshire by about A.D. 78. When they arrived in what is now Scotland, in the late 70's A.D., the Romans found British tribes living south of the rivers Clyde and Forth. These tribespeople spoke a Celtic language related to Welsh and Cornish. The Romans referred to the people north of the Clyde and Forth as Picts (painted people), arising from their habit of painting their skin. Evidence indicates that the Picts had lived in northern Scotland since about 700 B.C. or earlier. Their language resembled the Celtic spoken by the Britons to the south, but it also preserved elements of an earlier language not related to other Indo-European tongues.

Between 79A.D. and 84A.D., the Roman general Agricola led his forces into northern Britain past the Forth, into Pictish territory. The Romans won a great victory over the Picts at Mons Graupius. Following Agricola's recall to Rome in 84, the Romans withdrew southwards. In 120 A.D. they built Hadrian's Wall, stretching between the Tyne and the Solway Firth, separating the Romans from the native Britons. Then they built a turf barrier, the Antonine Wall, connecting the Forth and the Clyde. The Romans later withdrew still further south, at the same time leaving Romanized British tribes, such as the Votadini, to police Hadrian's Wall, which became their northern frontier.

During the Roman period Wales shared broadly the experience of other parts of highland Britain, but modern archaeological study has tended to moderate the traditional contrast drawn between military and civil zones. Mediterranean culture is best exemplified in southern Wales, where there were important Roman towns at Caerwent and Carmarthen and villas at a number of other sites. Remains elsewhere consist mainly of the roads and forts of a phase of military occupation that lasted to about AD 200. But at Caernarfon (Segontium) there was a continuous well-ordered settlement to about AD 400, and it is likely that civil influences were exerted much more widely than was once thought. Linguistic study suggests that the native language, known to scholars as Brittonic or Brythonic, was infused with Latin terms, though distinction needs to be made between borrowings of the period of Roman rule and the scholarly borrowings of subsequent periods. Early Welsh consciousness of a Roman heritage may owe a great deal to the Latinity sustained in later centuries by the Christian church.

The Romans imposed the most obvious changes thanks to their organisational superiority. With them came foreign soldiers, traders and slaves from across the empire, from Africa, Syria, Spain and Greece. Despite this, Britain's population remained substantially British. By A.D. 100 there were, surprisingly, a vast number of British serving overseas as soldiers in the Roman army.

Recent archaeological excavations have produced detailed biological evidence throwing light on production and consumption in the Roman-occupied areas. New crops and foodstuffs appeared together with new technologies. A number of new breeds of sheep were introduced which required shearing as opposed to plucking thus making shears a common tool of the new Romano-British farmer. Hay meadows appeared for the first time allowing greater control over animal feed and the introduction of large iron scythes which have been discovered on a number of sites.

With the Roman army and traders came more diverse plants bringing increased variety to the British diet, the majority of farmsteads growing coriander, cumin, fennel, dill, rosemary and even opium poppy. Imported exotic spices were introduced at this time.

Hill-forts - Caer Drewyn, Corwen, North Wales

Caer Drewyn Hill-Fort, Corwen, North Wales.   Photo: Dennis Williams

The ancient hill-fort of Caer Drewyn in Corwen in the district of Edeyrnion, North Wales was occupied two centuries before Christ by the Brythonic Celts and was one of over 600 in Wales. In A.D. 64, the Romans arrived in Edeyrnion under the command of Suetonius Paulinus, and under various commands remained here until the decline in the west of the Roman Empire circa A.D. 410. The Romans replaced the timber pallisade with stone walling and stone parapets. It is likely, though not certain, that they cultivated grapes on the south-facing slope, the name Trewyn being a corruption of Trewin (literal translation Wine Town).

Surprisingly, the Romans, ostensibly far advanced than most other civilizations in many ways, used mainly above ground granaries for threshed grain and suffered great losses to grain weevils and other pests. The ancient Celts occupying Caer Drewyn and other hill-forts had underground grain siloes or storage pits dug into the ground capped off with clay and each capable of storing some one to two tonnes of grain.

This type of storage was efficient due to the carbon dioxide given out by the grain acting as an insecticide thereby preserving it from one season to the next.

Suetonius Paulinus

Gaius Suetonius Paulinus was the Roman governor of Britain from 58-61 A.D. at the time of Boudicca's rebellion.

The earliest record of his career dates from before his time in Britain, when in the year 42 AD, during the reign of the Emperor Claudius in Rome, he suppressed a revolt in Mauretania and followed this leading his troops in the Atlas mountains of Algeria. His campaigns in Africa had taught him to tackle tough, independent-minded hill tribesmen such as the Silures and Deceangli of North Wales. He was promoted from the rank of praetor to that of legatus legionis in consequence. At around the same time Britain was invaded by Aulus Platius, with a force of some 20,000 men.

Suetonius was appointed governor of Britain in the year 58, by which time the area south-east of a line between the Wash and the Severn estuary was settled under Roman domination. However, the less stable south-west was putting up resistance against the Roman Second Legion, which had bases at Exeter, Gloucester and Cirencester. In the north-east, the Ninth Legion was based on Lincoln and Longthorpe, near Peterborough. The main force used by Suetonius for pushing his borders forward was that of the Fourteenth and Twentieth legions, centred on Chester.

The frontier between the settled lands and the military zone was the road now known as the Foss Way, which leads from Cirencester to Lincoln. Suetonius engaged in war against the Ordovices in Wales, launched an offensive against the Druids in Anglesey at the start of the campaign season of 61 A.D.. Here he was victorious, but, far to the south-east of Britain, in the rich, settled region around the capital, Colchester, rebellion erupted. The uprising endangered not only the province but also Paulinus's career.

Modern places names are used in describing what followed. The Iceni tribe, led by Boudicca, rose against the Romans and sacked Colchester. Suetonius, on learning of this potentially highly damaging event, hurried to London, with the Fourteenth and half of the Twentieth legions following him down Watling Street (now the A5 London to Holyhead road which runs through part of Edeyrnion, notably Glyndyfrdwy, Carrog and Corwen).

He ordered the Second Legion to move up to Bicester on his right flank, and the Ninth to attack on his left. But the British defeated the Ninth, and

Suetonius, deciding that both London and St Albans were impossible to defend, fell back along Watling Street, to meet up with his army at Towcester.

Just south of the town he took position in a defile, facing south-east with the road through the Wittlewood forest at his back. The British, denied the opportunity to outflank the Romans, attacked this narrow frontage head on. The professional efficiency of Suetonius's men won the day.

The aftermath was horrific. The governor's revenge on the rebels was so severe that he was recalled to Rome the following year. However, he was not disgraced, for he became a consul in 66 A.D. and in the civil war of 69, although he won a battle near Cremona, he found himself on the losing side in the war, but was granted a pardon. What became of him thereafter is not known.

Maximus Magnus, usurping Roman emperor who ruled Britain, Gaul, and Spain from AD 383 to 388. A Spaniard of humble origin, Maximus commanded the Roman troops in Britain against the tribes of northern Britain. In the spring of 383, Maximus is reported to have taken soldiers from North Wales into Europe though it is not clear what areas these troops were conscripted from.

CUNEDDA

Cunedda Wledig (Kuneda Wloedeg)
Father of the Welsh Nation

During the latter part of the fourth or possibly the early part of the fifth century, a vast army was making its way in a southwesterly direction from what is today the Lothian district of Scotland. The army itself being made up of Votadini Celts (Y Gododdin). Their destination was North Wales.

What reason could there be for such a warlike migration from the eastern part of the Scottish border country to the north of Wales? As to the mission itself there appears to be no doubt whatsoever - to rid North Wales of marauding invaders from Ireland who had settled along the Welsh coastline towards the end of the Roman occupation in the late 4th century; the mission itself established but more importantly, who was leading this army and at whose bequest? We can establish the former but there does appear to be some mystery as to the identity of the instigator.

Leading the army was none other than Cunedda Wledig (*Kuneda Wloedeg*), king of the north of Britain. Two names emerging over the years associated with requesting Cunedda and his vast army to engage against the Irish invaders are those of Vortigern and Maximus Wledig.

Originally it was thought that the Roman leadership had generated Cunedda's migration, probably in the Roman custom of *foederatio* - rewarding natives with land in return for military duty. However, more recent theories lean toward the idea that Vortigern, the pre-Arthurian, near-equivalent of a British high king from around 425 A.D., affected Cunedda's move. He was the chieftain who allegedly granted land to Anglo-Saxon-Jute mercenaries in return for their intervention against invading Picts from the north, a practice he escalated dramatically over the years of his leadership. As the army of the Roman empire disappeared from British soil, it seems more likely that Vortigern was the instigator of using Cunedda's war talents against the Irish, the Romans apparently being too preoccupied with returning to the continent to fight their own invaders. A further reason confirming Vortigern's role in this assignment was the fact that Maximus Wledig died in August 388, many years prior to Cunedda's offensive.

The journey from Manaw Gododdin to North Wales may well have proved enduring but did not compare to the journey which preceded this - one of 12,000 miles and a time-span exceeding 3,000 years.

IN SEARCH OF CUNEDDA

Who was Cunedda? Very little is known about the man, but various theories have attempted to fill in the blank spots of his life.

Historically, Cunedda became king of Gwynedd in North Wales (it must be noted that during this period of history the territory of Gwynedd covered the majority of North Wales) during the first half of the 5th century A.D. and founded a dynastic clan from which Welsh nobility has claimed their ancestry for centuries afterward. Tradition holds that Cunedda originated from the territory of Manau Gododdin, the region around what is now modern Edinburgh in southeast Scotland, and later migrated to North Wales. This movement was apparently designed to offer Cunedda land in return for ousting Irish raiders.

Cunedda was one among five important chieftains who were given the title Gwledig (or Wledig), which approximately means "landholder" in primitive Welsh. Because of its exclusivity, it could have eventually meant prince, ruler, even king. One of those other chieftains was Ceredig, a chieftain of Strathclyde, an important kingdom in what is now southwest Scotland, its capital in Dun Breatann, now Dumbarton, and the area still carries the name to this day. Once established in North Wales, Cunedda's kingdom became known as Gwynedd, comprising almost the whole of North Wales and not just the modern-day Gwynedd of North-west Wales.

At first glance, it is difficult to believe that the Celtic people who became the Cymry would have allowed an outside ruler to be thrust upon them unless he had met with their profound approval. Celtic custom practiced that leaders had to be approved by consensus as to their fitness to rule, not leaving such decisions strictly to hereditary fate. This view is especially important when we assume that even though the Roman leaders deprived the Celts of their native royalty during the occupation, there must have been remnants of local aristocracy and tribal chieftains still in Wales who were itching to regain the power their ancestors had lost.

Wales became fairly Romanized during the occupation; the most influence was exerted in the southern regions and around the northern coastline, though not as much as the rest of the island south of Hadrian's Wall. The Cymry retained much more of their native culture as did the northern Celts of Strathclyde, Manau Gododdin, and Cumbria, all people of the same ethnic stock who still shared similar customs and spoke the same language, in spite of four hundred years of occupation.

And therein lies a clue to Cunedda's acceptance. Could he have been a descendant of a pre-Roman Celtic king or prince of North Wales, and the most logical heir to the Welsh throne? Knowing the final conquest of North Wales was completed in 60 A.D., it is highly conceivable that refugees, possibly including some nobility, could have fled to Strathclyde and Manau Gododdin. The first Roman northern frontier was not established by the building of Hadrian's Wall until sixty years later as the Romans were well-occupied with revolts in other areas, including that of the renowned Boudicca. There would have been plenty of opportunity for escape to the north and generations of planning a return home.

Was Cunedda's move to North Wales purely greed-motivated, lusting for land, or was he seeking to restore his ancestors' rightful place? We are told that Cunedda's family consisted of eight sons and/or grandsons, among whom much of the land of Wales was split, each region taking its name from one of the sons. Although this organization may be more legend than fact, it does follow the medieval Welsh custom of gavelkind by dividing property among the male children of a family. We are also told that his grandfather was called Padarn Beisrudd (Paturnus of the Red Cloak), and the "red cloak" may have been a name indicating Roman officership. But Cunedda's name was Celtic, as were his ancestors prior to his grandfather, therefore Roman ancestry does not seem likely.

The common background and similarity of names in both Cunedda's and Ceredig's families indicate they could have been kinsmen or at least close allies. One of Cunedda's sons names was Ceredig. In those times, it appears that sons were named after grandfathers and uncles, but not their fathers, so in this instance, it may be logical to guess Ceredig the son was named for his kinsman from Strathclyde. The close ties Cunedda's family and people appear to have retained, coupled with the occupation's dissolution and Vortigern's offer of land, could well have nurtured a deep-seated desire to return to a Welsh homeland.

History so far is silent on any further facts regarding Cunedda's life. We can presume he was a capable military commander, a prodigious father, and well-organized, if his success at ousting the Irish and dividing Wales among his many sons is any indication. Unfortunately, because most knowledge of him and his times is lost due to language evolution, illiteracy, druidic bans on written documentation, and the destruction of war. With luck, however, perhaps archaeologists and historians will one day rediscover information that has been considered forever lost.

Lineage of Cunedda Wledig (The Imperator)

Also known as Kuneda Wloedig ap Edeyrn. He was the ruler of Manau Goutodin (Manaw Gododin) King of North Wales. Son of Aeternus

(Edeyrn), grandson of Padarn Beisrudd of the Red Robe ap Tegid and great-grandson of Doli ap Gwrddu of Britain.

Born c. 386 Died c. 445

His pedigree appears in the Jesus College MS 20 and other early Welsh genealogical tracts thus:Beli, Amalech, Ewein, Prydein, Dibun, Eimet, Anuueret,Gordofyn, Gordoli, Gorein, Cein, Genedawc, Iago, Tegyth, Padarn Beisrud, Edern, Cuneda.

However, the earlier pedigree in the Harleian MS 3859 gives a more accurate picture: Beli Magni, Amalech, Aballac, Eugein, Brithguein, Dubun, Oumun, Anguerit, Amguoloyt, Gurdumn, Dumn, Guordoli, Doli, Guorcein, Cein, Tacit, Patern Pesrut, Aetern, Cuneda. The older pedigree shows that a number of the generations given in the later ancestries are, in fact, duplications. Three of them simply add the prefix 'Guor-' on to each name and it has been suggested that this was part of some sort of bardic chant which helped people remember the names.

Cunedda, like many of his contemporaries, claimed descent from the Celtic gods Beli and Afallach, yet his immediate ancestors had Roman names: Aeternus, Paternus & Tacitus. They were probably leaders of the Votadini tribe and were on excellent terms with the Roman administration south of Hadrian's Wall probably forming part of a pro-Roman borderland buffer zone. Paternus' Red-Robe may even suggest the official purple garb of the Roman Administration.

The family continued thus:Cunedda Wledig (*the Imperator*), Cunedda's wife was Gwawl verch Coel Hen (*of 'Old King Cole' fame*) the marriage producing at least 12 children:-

Tybion, abt 417, Ysfael Gwron b. 418, Rhufon b. 419, Dunod, b. 420, Ceredig, b. 421, Afloeg b. 422, Einion Yrth, b. 423, Dogfael, b. 424, Edern abt 425, Tegeingl abt 426, Gwen abt 427. More unreliable sources give three further sons: Mael, abt 428 - Coel, abt 429 - Arwystl, abt 430.

A poem by Aneurin entitled *'Marwad Cunedda' (Death of Cunedda)* is a tribute to his life. When invited to rid north Wales of the Irish invaders this was done, according to Nennius with *'immense slaughter'*. Nennius c. 800 a Welsh antiquary who between 796 and about 830 compiled or revised the Historia Brittonum, a miscellaneous collection of historical and topographical information including a description of the inhabitants and invaders of Britain and providing the earliest-known reference to the British king Arthur.

Old King Cole

Old King Cole, to many of us a character associated with the traditional nursery rhyme, whereas in fact there are several candidates for this historical King Cole, or Coel, and one noteably linking him with Edeyrnion.

Geoffrey of Monmouth lists a King Cole in his Historia Regum Britanniae as a king of the Britons following the reign of King Asclepiodotus. The Welsh chronicles state further that his name was Coel Hen Godhebog.

David Nash Ford and Peter L. Kessler contend that Cole was *'Coel Hen, High King of Northern Britain'* who apparently lived around AD 350-420, during the time when the Romans withdrew their forces from Britain. He may have been the last of the Roman *'Duces Brittanniarum'* (Dukes of the Britons), and took over the northern capital at *Eburacum* (York) to rule over what had been the northern province of Roman Britain. Most of the Brythonic kings of north Britain, and many Welsh kings, would trace their descent from him — for example Rheged. He is also considered to be the father-in-law of Cunedda.

NB. If ever we required reasons to be proud of our local history then no better links exist to our past than the two Owain's of North Wales - Owain Gwynedd, who, in 1165, assembled on Caer Drewyn, Corwen, what has been described as the greatest Welsh army of the Medieval period, to prepare for battle against Henry II's invasion of Wales.

Secondly, Owain Glyndwr, probably the greatest of all the Welsh Princes. His constant warfares against Henry IV dominated his life but surprisingly we learn how he so very nearly became the father-in-law and grandfather of the King of England.

OWAIN GWYNEDD

King of Gwynedd

(Born c 1100 - died 1170)

Following many successful battles to strengthen his own borders in North Wales, Owain Gwynedd gained a noteable conquest by capturing Englefield (part of the old Flintshire containing the lands of Hope and English Maelor which bordered Chester). In response, Henry II mobilized a massive expedition with its objective *"to destroy all Welshmen"*.

It was on Caer Drewyn in Corwen that Owain Gwynedd encamped, having summoned a great army to await the arrival of Henry II. It is said there had never assembled an army so representative of the whole of Wales, the medieval chronicle *'Brut y Tywysogyon'* records the event as follows:-

"And when the king (Henry II) had thought that there were would be fighting against his castles which were in Tegeingl, he moved a host in great haste and came to Rhuddlan and encamped there for three nights. And after that he returned to England and gathered along with him a mighty host of the picked warriors of England and Normandy and Flanders and Anjou and Gascony and all Scotland; and he came as far as Oswestry, purporting to carry into bondage and to destroy all the Britons (at this period of history, the Welsh were the native Britons). And to meet him came Owain Gwynedd and Cadwaladr, sons of Gruffudd ap Cynan, and all the host of Gwynedd along with them, and the Lord Rhys ap Gruffudd and all Deheubarth along with him, and Owain Cyfeiliog and Iorwerth Goch ap Maredudd and the sons of Madog ap Maredudd and all Powys along with them, and the two sons of Madog ap Idnerth and all their might along with them. And all steadfastly united together they came

into Edeirnion, and they encamped at Corwen on Caer Drewyn."

The route Henry took, using Oswestry as a base, was to advance through the fairly open Ceiriog valley, with the intention to cross the Berwyn mountains to the upper part of the Dee valley. Finally, Henry's army reached the open mountain south of Corwen at Moel y Gwynt on the Berwyn range. Rain fell in torrents, great storms swept over the exposed heights of the moorland. The expedition was a complete tactical disaster due in part to logistical breakdown and inclement weather, but there can be no doubt the main reason for Henry's retreat on the Berwyn's was the guerilla resistance led by the might of Owain Gwynedd's army encamped in Corwen forcing Henry's attempt to collapse.

A medieval Welsh chronicler, described how, in 1165, he had seen the army of Owain Gwynedd encamped not only on Caer Drewyn in Corwen, but also on *"...ramparts of earth south and above Corwen, with an abundance of tents in Cynwyd".* It was further chronicled that following Henry's arrival at Shrewsbury, he marched onto Oswestry and from there through the Ceiriog valley. His army was greeted with a shower of arrows from an unseen enemy, and this considerably delayed his advance onto the Berwyns. It is probable that the *'unseen enemy'* was the one encamped at Cynwyd, for the journey from here to the Ceiriog Valley would be across the adjoining Berwyn moors. This skirmish delayed Henry's advance on to the Berwyn's in Corwen by some days and played a significant part in his disastrous bid to defeat Owain Gwynedd.

Owain was the second son of King Gruffudd ap Cynan of Gwynedd and Angharad, the daughter of Owain ap Edwin. His epithet is explained by the existence of another Owain ap Gruffudd, known as Owain Cyfeiliog.

He married, firstly, Gwladys, the daughter of Llywarch ap Trahaearn; and secondly, Christina, his cousin, the daughter of Goronwy ap Owain *'the Traitor,'* Lord of Tegeingle, to whom he remained constant despite the active disapproval of the Church. He had eight sons (Iorwerth, Rhun, Cynan, Iefan, Maelgwn, Madog, Ropert & Idwal) and two daughters (Gwenllian wife of Owain Cyfeiliog and another) by the first marriage; two sons (Dafydd and Rhodri) and one daughter (Angharad wife of Gruffudd Maelor I) by the latter. He also had another relationship with Pyfog of Ireland, by whom he had a son, Hywel.

As a young man in the 1120s, Owain was largely associated with his elder brother, Cadwallon, in restoring Gwynedd's prosperity on behalf of their ageing father. Together, they directed the military campaigns which added Meirionydd, Rhos, Rhufoniog and Dyffryn Clwyd to Gwynedd proper. Thus, at his accession to the throne, upon Gruffudd's death in 1137

- Cadwallon having died five years earlier - the groundwork for an impressive career had already been firmly set.

Political anarchy in England had already provided Owain the opportunity to combine his forces with those of Gruffudd ap Rhys and others. Together, they inflicted defeat on the Normans at Crug Mawr, in 1136, and temporarily occupied Ceredigion. Owain's campaigns in South Wales, however, were largely intended as a diversionary tactic designed to obscure his main objective of territorial consolidation in the North. Eventually, despite the opposition of Earl Ranulf of Chester and Prince Madog ap Maredydd of Powys, the area surrounding Mold submitted to him in 1146 and, three years later, Tegeingl and Iâl followed suit. By 1157, however, the situation over the border in England had changed considerably and Owain suffered his one and only decisive reversal at the hands of Henry II.

Though the English King's expedition to Gwynedd was militarily indecisive, it marked a new and positive stage in relations between the two Kingdoms. Deprived of Tegeingl and Iâl, Owain was forced to accept the return of his exiled brother, Cadwaladr, and offer him a share of power. However, with characteristic prudence and insight, Owain realised the great potential of a friendly relationship with the Plantagenet monarchy. He did homage to King Henry and seems to have agreed to change his status from '*King*' to mere '*Prince*'. Owain, made no further attempt to break his new-found feudal link with the English when, at the climax of his reign after the general Welsh uprising of 1165, he destroyed the royal strongholds of Tegeingl and re-established the power of Gwynedd along the Dee estuary. For Owain regarded himself as no ordinary vassal (as shown by his attitude to Episcopal elections in Bangor). He gave clear direction to the policies of his successors, enabling the Welsh Kings to take their place alongside the great feudal magnates of the time.

He is believed to have commissioned the propaganda text, *"The Life of Gruffydd ap Cynan"*, an account of his father's life. He died on 28th November 1170 and was buried in the cathedral at Bangor where his traditional tomb may still be seen. Following his death, civil war broke out between his sons, and a generation passed before Gwynedd was restored to its former glory.

During the year of 1080, some twenty years prior to the birth of Owain, at the time the princes of Gwynedd, Powys and South Wales were making a stubborn and determined stand against the invading Normans, his father, King Gruffudd ap Cynan, was betrayed by an act of treachery at Rug Hall in Corwen..

The prominent protagonists in this part of local history were three powerful earls, Hugh D'Avranches of Chester (*also known as Hugh Lupus*), Robert de Montgomerie and Hugh of Montgomerie, 2nd Earl of Shrewsbury (*also known as Hugh the Red*). Gruffudd ap Cynan was proving to be the sharpest thorn in the flesh of these earls. Having defeated their allies, Gruffudd ap Cynan gained support from most of Wales. The cunning earls, aiming to bring an end to the years of strife, called a truce, requesting Gruffudd ap Cynan to a rendezvous at Corwen to discuss terms. It was Meirion Goch of Llyn, who informed Gruffudd of the request of his presence to meet the Earls at Rug and duly arrived at Rug.

On hearing that the prince was at Rug the Earls came with a group of soldiers under the pretence of visiting him. Meirion Goch persuaded Gruffudd to go with a small guard to meet them, unaware of the kidnapping plot by the earls, and was seized and carried off to Chester Castle. He was kept there for twelve years in chain and irons. The guards that accompanied Gruffudd were likewise taken prisoners, and after having been barbarously treated, and their right-hand thumbs cut off, were then allowed to go free.

A Corwen youth, Kynrig (Cwyrig) Hir of Iâl, witnessed the event and bided his time to avenge the treachery, although it would be almost twelve years before he was successful in assisting with Gruffudd's escape from Chester. This was carried out with cool precision. Under the pretence of buying necessities, he took an occasion whilst the jail-keepers were feasting and no doubt up to the gills in ale, carried away his Prince, still laden with irons on his back, to a place of safety prior to returning to Rug.

OWAIN GLYNDWR

c.1359 - 1416

The last native born Prince of Wales

OWYNUS DEI GRATIA PRINCEPS WALLIAE
'Owain, by the grace of God, Prince of Wales'.

The great seal of Owain Glyn Dwr only survives in a single impression attached to his 1404 treaty with Charles VI of France.

On the obverse, Owain is shown enthroned beneath a canopy of state, holding a sceptre, but with no crown. A lawyer by training, here he represents the role of a king as the giver of justice. As in French royal seals, angels hold up his cloth of majesty, which shows the lions rampant of Gwynedd. His feet rest on two more lions, and two wolf heads spring from the arms of his throne.

On the reverse, Owain appears on horseback as the warrior and feudal leader he certainly was - this time with a crown on his helmet. The Welsh dragon appears on both his helmet, and on the warhorse's head.

During the latter part of the 13th century, Gruffudd ap Madog, the Prince of Northern Powys died leaving his lands to be divided between his four sons in accordance with the ancient laws of gavelkind. These lands included Glyndyfrdwy and Cynllaith. The old laws of Wales under Hywel Dda had been replaced by the Statute of Rhuddlan of 1284 which demanded allegiance from the Welsh and the estates were divided on the English plan as shires. So rather than the tenure of the lands being passed onto his sons, these passed on to the new ruling families and divided among the Earl of Surrey, Roger Mortimer of Chirk, and Eleanor of Castile who was Edward I's Queen.

One of the sons of Gruffudd ap Madog, Gruffudd Fychan, appeased the Earl of Surrey by some means, and consequently became the 'tenant at will' of the lands of Glyndyfrdwy, which were his by right of inheritance. On his passing the estates reverted to the Crown, and both Glyndyfrdwy and Cynllaith are mentioned in Queen Eleanor's will in 1290. The lordship of the area had fallen to Reginald de Grey of Ruthin, but Thomas of Macclesfield was appointed as guardian of the lands of Gruffudd Fychan, although it is not known how these territories had once again become hereditary. Subsequently, Madog, the young son of Gruffudd Fychan was installed as baron of the Welsh March in 1300, owning the lands of Glyndyfrdwy and Cynllaith.

After a short period Madog died, leaving his young son Gruffudd to become a ward of John le Strange, the young boy's father-in-law. Following the death of le Strange the young Gruffudd's inheritance fell into the hands of one Edmund Hakluyt, and this guardianship was subsequently bought by the Mortimers of Chirk. A legal battle ensued when Gruffudd was old enough, resulting with him winning back all his father's lands and became a baron in his own right by order of King Edward II in 1321.

In turn, the estates were passed to his son, Gruffudd Fychan the Younger. His marriage to Helen came with a dowry of rich estates in South Wales, Bangor Iscoed near Wrexham and Gwynionydd in Cardiganshire. The union of this marriage produced two sons, Owain (Glyndwr) and Tudur ap Gruffudd.

Owain Glyndwr's father had died by 1370 and he would have been considered too young to have succeeded his estates. There is a strong possibility that he and the estates were taken into the custody of Sir David Hanmer, he himself being a distinguished and accomplished lawyer is likely to have insisted on a basic legal education for Owain, his ward and his future son-in-law. The chronicler of St Albans comments that Owain spent a period of his youth as an apprentice at law at Westminster.

Without doubt the most famous son of Edeyrnion and probably the whole of Welsh history, much ambiguity surround the date and place of the birth of Owain Glyndwr although the year is now widely accepted as being 1359. More mystery surround his death and even more the place of his burial; although not recorded, it is nevertheless acknowledged that the year was 1415. The Peniarth Manuscript at the National Library of Wales, Aberystwyth records:

"1415: Owen went into disappearance on St Mathew's day in harvest-time and thereafter his disappearance was not known. A great many say that he died; the seers maintain that he did not" (*St Mathew's day is September 21st*). A contemporary of Glyndwr's was Adam of Usk who also confirms 1415 as the year of his death. Writing on Glyndwr's death he mentions two pointers of note in that Glyndwr had been in hiding for some years prior to his death and also that the location of his grave was kept a

secret to protect it from ill-boding enemies.

The Panton Manuscript at the National Library of Wales quotes on page 58b: "*Death put an end to Owain's life and misery upon the eve of St Mathew A.D. 1415. Some say he died at his daughter Scudamore's, others at his daughter Monnington's house. Both of them harboured him in his low forlorn condition, they say he was fain to go up and down disguised in a shepherd's habit into his daughter and other friends houses.*"

There is even a suggestion that John Kent, a bard and priest patronized by the Scudamores, was Owain Glyndwr's assumed identity.

Several places have been mentioned as being his resting place, but I, perhaps with some bias, make the supposition that this is in the grounds of the Church of St Mael and St Sulien in Corwen, which is discussed further in this chapter. Recently, some interesting pieces of scripts were discovered in the Harleian MS. (see page 85)

His inheritance consisted of two estates, namely Glyndyfrdwy and Cynllaith. These two estates were separated from each other by the Berwyn range of mountains. Many historians state the real home of Owain Glyndwr as that of Llansantffraid Glyndyfrdwy, where the river Dee meanders through from the rural district of Edeyrnion to the plain of industrial Maelor. The name Glyndwr is merely a shortened form of Glyn Dyfrdwy. His other home, on the south side of the Berwyns, was at Sycharth, near Llansilin, and to the south-east of Corwen.

A celebrated bard of that time, Iolo Goch, described Sycharth in great detail; the manor was surrounded by a moat over which a bridge led to the imposing gate-house. On the green hill were timber houses, built on pillars, which resembled the cloisters of Westminster. The roofs were tiled; the chimneys smoked, indicating the continual activity within as lavish meals were prepared for the many guests who frequently savoured Glyndwr's hospitality. Close by stood a mill, among other small buildings such as a stone pigeon-house. There was a rabbit warren and a heronry, and the whole complex of buildings exuded warmth, joy and a welcome from Owen's delightful wife.

Whilst attempting to establish the date and place of Owain's birth, his death and burial place may well present difficulties, establishing dwelling-places of his estates should have fewer. It has long been believed that Owain Glyndwr's Edeyrnion's estate was in the village of Glyndyfrdwy. However, it is more than likely that the village of Glyndyfrdwy and the parish of Llansantffraid Glyndyfrdwy, comprising of the villages of Glyndyfrdwy and Carrog, added to some confusion in establishing the true whereabouts of Glyndwr's estate. His estate at Glyndyfrdwy is reported in Rees Davies's "*The Revolt of Owain Glyndwr*" as being composed of his farm dwelling of Rhuddallt, a mill, pasture and sheep-runs. However, the dwelling of Rhuddallt was a township in the vicinity of where today stands the village of Ruabon, located between Offa's and Wat's Dyke, and is indeed quoted in a number of texts as being the real birthplace of Owain Glyndwr. Therefore long established links with the village of Glyndyfrdwy as his Edeyrnion residence must be thrown into doubt. Helen Allday writes ("*Insurrection in Wales*") that "*...the family estates were centred at Carrog and Sycharth*", and in addition to this a number of texts mention Prince Henry's murderous deed of destroying by fire Glyndwr's homes at Sycharth and Carrog, emphasising the probability that there was no dwelling in the village of Glyndyfrdwy itself.

His home at Carrog on the north-side of the Berwyns has not been mentioned in any detail except that where it stood, approximately a quarter of a mile outside of Llidiart-y-Parc between the river Dee and the A5, a lodge was on the mount itself surrounded by a moat. This dwelling place in Carrog is often referred to as a 'fine lodge in the park' but this raises the question for me that if the remains of the mound are considered to be the original dimension this would throw doubt onto its capacity to victual a household, and so a first impression would beg the question 'what was the purpose of such a small mound?' To help answer this I refer to the Ordnance Survey map (Sheet SJ04/14 for a fuller description:

This displays the mound on the north-side of the A5 road and is described as 'Moat'; the description 'Owain Glyndwr's Mount' is highlighted on the south-side of the A5 road. Approaching the mound on the A5 from either direction and you travel on the cutting made by Thomas Telford in 1815 to take the road through a high banked mound on the south side which I consider to be the main part of the 'mound' and one of such dimension as to befit a household, its troops and certainly one in which to entertain. The site itself was considered by Dr E.A. Neaverson in his book "Medieval Castles of North Wales" (1956) to be one where stood a Norman castle so this would support the theory that the original mound was much larger.

A sixteenth-century chronicler and poet, John Leland (1503-1552), described by many during his lifetime as "the father of local English and Welsh history" completely ignored that the mound in Carrog was the location of Owain's manor. He clearly identifies Rhagad (Rhagatt), on the site of the post-medieval Rhagatt Hall further up river, as the real manor of Owain Glyndwr, although some sources maintain this was linked to Tudur, brother of Owain.

In addition to this, his prison house (Carchardy Owain Glyndwr) was in the village of Carrog, and Thomas Pennant (Hanes Owen Glyndwr, Tywysog Cymru) writes "*The prison where Owen confined his captives was not far from his house....*" There is of course the question of Pennant's source but this would make sense to have his prison house near to his residence as the distance between the villages of Glyndyfrdwy and Carrog would have made travel demanding between these two points in that period, given the terrain and the possible hazard this would present.

There is also a reference to Erw Lâs as to where Owain held court and was on the site of what is today Penybont farm which stands on the south side of the river on the road between Llidiart-y-Parc and the village of Carrog, thereby linking the 'tomen', his court and prison-house within close proximity.

Like most of the Welsh gentry of the Middle Ages, Owain Glyndwr was learned in law, having studied at the Inns of Court in Westminster. In the early part of the fifteenth century, there was a truce in the Hundred Years' War. Were it not for this, it is highly likely that he would have fought in France, thus denying him the opportunity of leading the rebellion during the insurrection in Wales, the event Owain Glyndwr will be most remembered for, leading a large army in the last Welsh war of independence, '*The Rebellion of Owain Glyndwr*'.

The immediate cause of the rising in Wales was a personal quarrel between Owain Glyndwr and Lord Grey of Ruthin, who coveted some of Owain's territories which bordered on his own. This emanated from the English feudal law of 'escheat'. In effect, this was a compulsory eviction of free tenants from well worked fertile lands to rain drenched mountainsides. An example of this law enforced by Lord Grey was the eviction of farming families from the very fertile Vale of Clwyd to the Hiraethog mountains some 1500ft above sea level.

Anticipating an attack from Lord Grey's army, Glyndwr took the offensive. Having summoned his brother Tudur, his eldest son and his wife's brothers, their first act was to proclaim Owain Glyndwr as Prince of Wales in September 1400. The movement of 1400 was carefully planned. From September 18th to the 23rd Owain and supporters attacked Ruthin, Denbigh, Rhuddlan, Flint, Holt, Oswestry and Welshpool.

Meanwhile, Henry IV's army, on its way home from Scotland to Shrewsbury, was diverted and galvanized into action for a lightning campaign into North Wales. Reasserting their control in Ruthin within ten days of the rebellion, the English authorities ordered the execution of eight of Glyndwr's supporters on the 28th September whilst hanging, drawing and quartering Gronw ap Tudur, dispatching the quarters to four border towns to break the will and to instill fear into any would be rebel.

By the summer of 1401 the situation had deteriorated to such an extent that North Wales was being besieged by a force of an army of more than five hundred, organized at Chester, strengthened by a large contingent based on Cae'r Drewyn in Corwen before marching onwards through Bala and reaching Harlech in the early autumn to relieve the original force.

The barons of Edeirnion,. Dinmael, Rug, Hendwr, Crogen and Cilan, linked to Owain Glyndwr by ties of descent via the stock of Bleddyn ap

Cynfyn, the founding father of the dynasty of Powys, joined forces raiding Harlech and it was from the ranks of their tenants that the bulk of the army was formed.

Towards the latter end of 1401 two leaders of the attack on Conway Castle surrendered themselves to the Prince of Wales at Chester which was followed by the desertion of a number of men from Carmarthenshire and Cardiganshire, all finally accepting a pardon from the king.

Early in the spring of 1402, an approaching comet lit up the skies of North Wales. Remarkable for its splendour and visible for several weeks, it was dragon-shaped and pointed in an easterly direction towards England. We must remember that in these Middle Ages, inexplicable lights were often interpreted as messages from either ancient gods or the Almighty. The people of Wales could only offer one explanation - 'it was viewed as either a warning of disaster or heralding some great event'. The Bayeux Tapestry commemorating the Battle of Hastings clearly shows Halley's comet glowing brightly, although following the comet's orbit of 1006, it was 1081 before the next. Those who observed the dragon-shaped comet saw this great light as one heralding the rise of their own Saviour, the Lord of Glyndyfrdwy, perhaps one in which the Welsh could emulate the victorious Normans, and certainly an opportunity to be freed from their bondage to the English.

Once they had gathered a small but powerful force, they ravaged Denbigh and Flint, set fire to Oswestry and plundered Welshpool. Ruthin was the last town to be attacked. That day, Owain Glyndwr's army lit a beacon which spread the length and breadth of Wales.

The revolt was only just beginning. Welsh scholars at the Universities of Oxford and Cambridge left their studies and went home to fight alongside their fellow countrymen. Welsh labourers in England threw up their jobs to return to Wales as news of the revolt spread. Welsh mercenaries were coming home from France and from the distant East. Wales now had a leader. Owain Glyndwr was their defender, protector of the common people, the incarnation of their love of country. He had given Wales national unity, a parliament and a university.

Following his victory at Ruthin, Owain Glyndwr took Lord Grey prisoner. Also, during a trip to Radnorshire to rouse the Welsh in that area, Glyndwr captured Edmund Mortimer who had advanced against him with an army of Herefordshire levies and Welsh archers. Mortimer's alliance was won over by marrying him to Owain's daughter Catrin. Along with Edmund Mortimer and Percy, Earl of Northumberland, Owain Glyndwr was instrumental in forming the new boundaries of Wales, thus extending the old boundaries demarcated by Offa's Dyke.

The repressive laws that Parliament, under Henry, hurled against the Welsh, possibly the first ever form of apartheid, included the yoking of

Englishmen who married Welsh women; no Englishman in Wales was to be convicted except by an Englishman; Welshmen were not to assemble for any purpose, nor carry arms or wear armour in town, market, church or on the highway. The Welsh were also barred from holding any office.

In the early part of 1403, the sixteen year old Prince Hal, later to become Henry V, was appointed by his father as Royal Deputy in Wales, which placed troops from the Border counties at his disposal. Eager to gain the initiative over Glyndwr, he proceeded to lead a vigorous attack on the homes of his adversary. In the May he had marched from Shrewsbury to Sycharth and Owain Glyndwr's home, along with the surrounding estates were burnt to the ground. The young Prince and his army then marched onwards over the Berwyns to Carrog where the home on the Mound was demolished. Tenants of Owain's were taken prisoner and executed as suspected sympathisers; innocent or guilty, no mercy was shown.

Incensed by young Hal's butchery, he was given inadvertent assistance by renewed activity in Scotland, which necessitated the presence of Henry IV and Hal. Towards the latter end of 1403, Owain Glyndwr's forces greatly increased. With French allies he attacked the castles along the coast from Beaumaris to Cardiff, and, apart from castles that were too strongly defended, Owain Glyndwr was complete master of Wales.

Following further victories at Harlech and Aberystwyth, he summoned a parliament to the town of Machynlleth. He later summoned another parliament, this time at Harlech. Both parliaments were attended by delegates from all over Wales, the first and last parliaments in Welsh history - although we do have the Welsh Assembly but which presently has no tax-raising powers as that of a full parliament. Nothing has been discovered which chronicled the transactions of the parliament, but he is supposed to have been crowned Prince of Wales in the presence of his loyal supporters and representatives from Wales, Ireland, Scotland, France and Spain.

In August 1405, Owain Glyndwr was further encouraged by news that a force of three thousand French had disembarked at Milford Haven. Together with his French allies, Glyndwr marched through Haverfordwest and Tenby to Carmarthen, which they duly captured. Having taken Cardigan, they moved on from the West of Wales passing through South Wales until they were within a few miles of Worcester, where Henry was awaiting reinforcements.

Realising that he was in hostile territory, Glyndwr retreated to the mountains with his French allies. The hard winter that followed influenced the majority of the French to return to their own country, with the remainder leaving the following year.

In 1406 Owain's vision for a Wales with two universities and independent Welsh Church was taken a step further with the withdrawal of support for the Roman papacy transferring ecclesiastical allegiance to the Avignonese Pope. Although this marked the turning tide for Owain's dreams he and his supporters were still capable of leading hit and run raids in north-east Wales. His forces however were diminished by the departure of the French troops and despite the apologies of the French for their insignificance, no further aid was received from this quarter and any hope of a similar contribution from his allies in Scotland were dealt a blow in the March when the heir to the Scottish throne was captured by the English.

By now the English government were pursuing a more ruthless policy towards the rebellion in Wales and their anger and frustration was marked by allocating 5,000 men to the prince of Wales, which despite his reluctance to discharge his duties was given large amounts of money for this duty.

The dallying by the prince did not however diminish the vigour of the English in their push to take the initiative from Owain Glyndwr. In February 1406 the garrison at Caernarfon was quadrupled and the rebels' ships were destroyed by a large naval force, the objective here to isolate Anglesey by reasserting English authority. Many soldiers were strategically placed on the Menai Straits to thwart any would be attempt by Owain's rebels. By early December the Anglesey court had re-convened with tax collection resuming normality. This show of power meant Anglesey had given up its resolve and the rebellion showed signs of crumbling. Many of Owain's allegiances submitted to Henry. Further aid from Charles IV of France did not materialise, and compatriots deserted at an alarming rate causing further decline.

Owain Glyndwr had now reached the zenith of his power, and steadily his influence declined. In 1406, many of his allegiances submitted to Henry. Further aid from Charles IV of France did not materialise, and compatriots deserted at an alarming rate causing further decline.

During the summer of 1407, Prince Henry besieged Aberystwyth and the castle fell the following year. In the year 1409 Harlech castle followed the fate of Aberystwyth. As these were the two castles Owain Glyndwr had made his headquarters, he now had no place in which to rally an army to further the insurrection. It was here his son-in-law Edmund Mortimer was killed. Owain's wife Margaret, and some of his daughters who were there, were taken prisoners to London.

Prince Henry who in 1413 became King Henry V, extended to Owain the hand of friendship, with the promise of a free pardon for himself and his followers. This was never accepted by Owain Glyndwr, though the reason for this was never known: possibly his health declined or, more probably, it was pride. It is likely that Owain Glyndwr died during 1415, as no event of his life is chronicled following this period. He had been the first, and indeed, according to many historians, the only Welsh prince to command wide support from every part of Wales.

It is not certain when and where Owain Glyndwr died, nor where his grave is to be found. The most favoured location amongst historians mention Monnington in Herefordshire as the place where he died. It is true that of Owain's daughters, Alice married John Scudamore and Margaret married Roger Monnington of Monnington. Both Scudamore and Monnington had estates in Herefordshire.

However, two ingenious signs indicate that he may be buried within the grounds of the Church of St Mael and St Sulien in Corwen, possibly where Owain first attended for worship. One is that he is buried near the Priest's Door in the church. On the lintel above the door on the south wall of the same church is inscribed the shape of a medieval sword (below). Is it possible that Owain Glyndwr made this inscription personally? More likely however is that possibly it was inscribed by either one of his followers or a local stone mason of the time to mark the place of his burial.

The second sign comes from the tapered granite cross shaft or cromlech which stands alongside the footpath at the south west of Corwen church which is mounted in a stone socket. Near the top of the shaft is an embossed carving of a small dagger. This again could indicate that this site is the burial ground of Owain Glyndwr. Both pre-Celtic and Celtic burial chambers for warriors consisted of vertical granite slabs surmounted by a capstone, and covered with a mound of earth. This was a symbol of the mystery of death and rebirth. Is it therefore possible that where only one granite shaft stands, that this marks the burial place of one warrior only - that of Owain Glyndwr? Our ancient Indo-European ancestors demonstrated archaeologically the arrival of the "pit grave" culture, which buried its dead in shafts, or barrows. A nobleman would be buried with his ceremonial dagger engraved on the shaft, reinforcing the hypotheses that the remains of Owain Glyndwr rest in Corwen.

However, a recent publication, *"Owain Glyndwr - A Casebook"* (2013) by Michael Livingston (Associate Professor at The Citadel, The Military College of South Carolina) and John K. Bollard (Medieval Welsh scholar) highlights one interesting discovery from the Harleian Manuscripts of Oxford.

This came about in quite an extraordinary way; a Venetian, Tito Livio Frulovisi, travelled to England in 1436 and under the employ of Humphrey, Duke of Gloucester, Frulovisi composed an influential biography of the duke's late brother, King Henry V. The completed manuscript, *"Vita Henrici Quinti"* was translated years later into many European languages including that of Middle-English in the year 1513. This translation by an unknown author is preserved in two extant manuscripts: MS Bodley 966 and MS Harley 35. The original text was amended by the inclusion of text from the Harley manuscript with a unique report of Owain Glyndwr's death. This text in Harley 35 detailed that Owain Glyndwr died on the hill of Lawton's Hope in Herefordshire in 1415, although no other such text has as yet been discovered which would corroborate this statement. That said, has to be the first ever written evidence discovered detailing Glyndwr's death.

No other reference has been discovered to pinpoint if this is where Owain drew his final breath. Does this give us cause to believe this gives us that final link? Is it possible it lends credence to other texts which state he died and was laid to rest in Herefordshire?

I still lean towards the hope of discovering that this should be in Corwen, as the following text is found within the publication of the book *"The Story of the Nations (Wales)"*, the eminent Welsh historian Sir Owain M. Edwards, states that "Owain himself probably lies at Corwen...." However, I find it disappointing that such a scholar should make such a claim without elaboration.

The Royal Commission on ancient monuments refer to the cross shaft as the 'remains of one of the crosses which are generally regarded as dating from the 9th century, so date wise this theory is most certainly feasible. These crosses are found to have been erected in various parts of the ancient kingdom of Mercia, the example at Corwen probably the furthest western extension of this type'. The actual cross-head has sadly disappeared, and due to that indiscriminating enemy of time, the interlaced Celtic pattern at what was the neck, has slowly eroded, but is still definable.

Owain married Margaret Hanmer of Flint, possibly in 1383 when he was twenty four years old. There are references to six sons - Gruffydd, Madog and Maredudd, all of whom where involved in the rebellion, plus three others, Thomas, John and David. There were several daughters also, but it is not clear whether there were five or six. In various chronicles it mentions Isabel (who married Adda ap Iorwerth Ddu), Alice, Margaret, Catrin, Janet and Jane. It is not clear whether Jane and Janet are one and the same.

OWAIN GLYNDWR SO NEARLY BECAME FATHER-IN-LAW AND GRANDFATHER TO THE KING OF ENGLAND

Catrin, daughter of Owain Glyndwr, married Sir Edmund Mortimer on 30 November 1402 who had avowed his allegiance to his new father-in-law.

During 1399 Henry, Duke of Lancaster decided to take the crown of England arguing that Richard II, through his misgovernment, had rendered himself to be unworthy of being King. However, the heir presumptive was a young Edmund Mortimer the 5th Earl of March, who had descended from Edward III's second son whilst Henry's father was Edward's third son, the younger Edmund being a nephew of Sir Edmund, the son-in-law of Owain Glyndwr.

The young Earl of March had been taken into the protective custody of Henry IV along with his brother Roger. Soon after this Roger died presumed killed by Henry IV. Afraid, following his brother's death, the Earl of March was never able to build enough of a power base to challenge the crown. With the death of the heir presumptive, Sir Edmund Mortimer, if he had lived would have been the real heir to the throne and his children by Catrin Glyndwr would have inherited the throne of England.

The tapered granite cross shaft stands alongside the footpath at the south-west of Corwen church mounted in a stone socket. Near the top of the shaft is an embossed carving of a small dagger (as seen inset enlarged photograph).

A Celtic warrior's burial ground was marked with a vertical shaft. Could this be the site of the burial place of Owain Glyndwr?

Photo: Pearl Williams

On the lintel above the door on the south wall of the same church is inscribed the shape of a medieval sword. It is possible that Owain Glyndwr made this inscription personally.

Photo: Pearl Williams

We are ever in the process of becoming.

CELTIC BLESSING

May the road rise up to meet you
May the wind be always at your back
May the sun shine warm upon your face
May the rain fall soft upon your fields
And until we meet again
May God hold you in
The palm of His hand

BENDITH GELTAIDD

Boed ir ffordd godi i'th gyfarfod
Boed yr awel o hyd i dy gefn
Boed gwres yr haul yn tywynnu'n dy wyneb
Boed y glaw'n dyner ddisgyn ar dy diroedd
A hyd y dydd cawn eto gwrdd
Boed i Dduw dy gynnal
Ym mhalmwydd Ei law.

Welsh translation: Megan Williams (2005)

Acknowledgements

i. The chapter Archaeological Analyses, paragraphs 2, 3, 4, 5, 6, 7, 9 and 15 are extracts from "The Tribes of Britain", by David Miles,(2005), ISBN 0-297-83086-4 and reproduced by kind permission of Weidenfeld & Nicolson, Orion Books Ltd.

ii. The chapter Owain Glyndwr, Paragraphs 18, 19, 20, 21, 27, 29, 33 and 34 are extracts taken from "The Revolt of Owain Glyndwr" by Davies, R. R. (1995) ISBN 0-19-820508-2 and reproduced by kind permission of Oxford University Press.

Bibliography

Allday, D. Helen	*"Insurrection in Wales",* Lavenham Press
Armit, Ian	*"Tempus", 1998*
Baldia, Maximilian O.,	*"The Corded Ware / Single Grave Culture*
Baucum, Walter	*"Tracing the Tribe of Dan"*
Brut Y Tywysogion	
Davidii, Yair	*"Lost Israelite Identity"*
Davidii, Yair	*"The Exile"*
Davis-Kimbell, Jeannine	*"Warrior Women: An Archaeologist's search for history's hidden heroines"*
Davies, Dr John	*"Mythology of the Ancient Druids"*
Davies, R.R.	*"The Revolt of Owain Glyndwr", Oxford University Press*
Edwards, Charles	*"Hanes y Fydd - 1675"*

Edwards, Owen M.   *"Story of the Nations" 1901*

Ellis, Peter   *"The Ancient World of the Celts"*

Encyclopædia Britannica Library   *"Cimmerian", Micropaedia, Vol. 3, p.321,15th Edition*
Encyclopædia Britannica Library   *"Ancient Iran"*
Encyclopædia Britannica Library   *"Bronze Age"*
Encyclopædia Britannica Library   *"Cremation"*
Encyclopædia Britannica Library   *"Iron Age"*
Encyclopædia Britannica Library   *"Indo-European Language and Sanskrit"*
Encyclopædia Britannica Library   *"Workhouse"*

Evans, D. Gareth   *"A History of Wales, 1815-1906",* University of Wales Press.

Filppula, Markku, Klemola, Juhani
and Pitkänen, Heli   *"The Celtic Roots of English"*

Gamkrelidze, Thomas V.,
and Ivanov V.V., 1990   *"The Indo-European Super-Family of Languages" Scientific American 1990*

Gardner, Sir Laurence   *"Nexus Magazine, Volume 6"*

Gimbutas, Marija   *"Hypotheses on North Pontic culture"*

Gregory, Donald   *"Wales Before 1536" Gwasg Carreg Gwalch*

Haggett, P.   *"Geography: A Modern Synthesis", Harper & Row, 1979*

Henry, John & Parker, James   *"Our British Ancestors: Who and What Were They?*

Jones, Sir William

lecture to the Royal Asiatic Society of Bengal

Kingsbury, Bill

"Khazars, Picts, Scotland"

Laessoe, Jorgen

"Who Were the Cimmerians, and Where Did They Come From?"

Laing, Lloyd & Jennifer

"Art of the Celts", Thames and Hudson Ltd.

Layard, Sir Austen Henry

"Discoveries in the ruins of Assyria and Babylon"

Livingston, Michael &
Bollard, John K.

"Owain Glyndwr: A Casebook" (2013)

Mackenzie, D.

"Human Geography"

Mallory, J.P.

The Oxford Introduction to Proto-Indo-European World

Megalommitis, Cosmas

"The Scientific Approach to the Ten Tribes of Israel"

Miles, David

"Tribes of Britain"

Moore, Thomas
von Miklosich Franz,

"History of Ireland"
"Romany Language"

Moses, Grace,

"The Welsh Lineage of John Lewis (1592-1657)" 1992

Neaverson, Dr E.

"Mediaeval Castles of North Wales"

Pennant, Thomas

"Hanes Owen Glyndwr, Tywysog Cymru"

Piggott, Stuart

"Scotland's Hidden History", 1982

Piotrovsky, Boris	*"Assyrian and Cimmerians"*
Price, T. Douglas	*"Strontium Isotopes and Human Migration"*
Rice, Tamara Talbot	*"Scythians and Cimmerians in southern Russia"*
Roberts, L.G.A.	*"identical Welsh parallel phrases for the Hebrew original"*
Williams, D.W.	*"The Royal Tribes of Wales"* *2016 Create Space, N.C., USA*
Williams, G.A.,	*"When Was Wales", Penguin Books, 1985*
Yorke, Philip,	*"The Royal Tribes of Wales" 1799*

I also wish to acknowledge the following academics and scholarly papers:-

Anne Kristensen, Danish linguistic scholar

Dr Jeaninne Davis-Kimbell - Scythian discoveries

Edward Lhuyd - curator of the Ashmolean Museum in Oxford - A branch of Indo-European had been identified in 1707) who recognised the relationship between Welsh, Irish, Scottish, Gaelic and Breton

Franz von Miklosich - Austrian Philologist

Brittanic Hebraisms academic papers which identify a number of Welsh Cambro-Brittanic Hebraisms in which whole phrases in Welsh can be closely paralleled by whole phrases in Hebrew.

INDEX

Indo-European	30, 31
London	80
Mael	67
Neolithic tribes	40
North America	38
Oswestry	78
Spain	30
Urartu	36
A5 London to Holyhead road	62
A5 road	76
Aballac	67
Aberdeen	53
Aberystwyth	79, 80
Adam of Usk	74
Adda ap Iorwerth Ddu	82
Aegean area	45
Aetern	67
Aeternus	67
Afallach	67
Afghanistan	4, 9
Afloeg	67
Africa	48, 60
Afroasiatic	26
Agathyrsai	4, 10, 11, 13, 14, 55
Agricola, Roman General	59
Akatziri	13
Albani	11
Alice	82
Allday, Helen	76
Alps	38
Amalech	67
America	22
Amguoloyt	67
Amuru	18
Anatolia	4, 9, 18, 26
ancient Britain	5
Ancient Sumerian	23
Aneirin	11, 53, 55
Aneurin	67
Angharad, mother of Owain Gwynedd	70
Angles	11
Anglesey	62, 80
Anglian	53
Anglo-Saxon	11, 36
Anglo-Saxon-Jute mercenaries	64
Anglo-Saxon. Northern	53
Anguerit	67
Anjou	69

Annales Cambriae	29
Anne Kristensen	21
Antonine Wall	55
Antonine wall	56
Antonine Wall	60
Anuueret,Gordofyn	67
Arab	13
Armenia	18, 21, 26
Armorica	54
Arthur, British king	67
Arwystl	67
Aryan	9, 21, 34
Aryans	27
Asclepiodotus, King	68
Ashmolean Museum Oxford	27
Asia	7, 14, 55
Asia Minor	9, 21, 22
Asia, Centrala	42
Asia, western	58
Asiatic Society	5
Assyria	18, 18, 21, 36, 38
Assyrian	11, 13, 19, 20, 21, 21, 35, 37
Assyrian Empire	11, 22, 28
Assyrians	17, 17, 35, 38
Atlantic	20
Aulus Platius	62, 62
Austria	42, 47
Avebury	29
Avignonese Pope, allegiance to	80
Babylon	22, 35
Babylonian	28
Balkans	18, 36
Baltic	27
Baltic Sea	11
Baltic Seashore	11
Balts	10
Bangor	71
Bangor Iscoed	74
Barbarians	11
Batavians	59
Bavaria	47
Bayeux Tapestry	78
Beaker folk	5
Beaker people	40, 40
Beaumaris	79
Bede	11, 55
Belgae	38
Belgium	46, 50
Beli	67

Beli Magni   67
Bell Beaker   47
Bell Beaker culture   46
Bell-Beaker   41
Bell-Beaker culture   58
Bengal   5
Bernaccia   56
Bernician Angles   57
Berwyn Mountains   6
Berwyn mountains   70, 79
Berwyn range   75
Bicester   62
Bit Humria   21
Black Sea   11, 15, 16, 20, 20, 39
Bleddyn ap Cynfyn   78
Bollard, John K.   81
Borders   55
Boudicca   62, 62, 66
Breton   27, 54
Britain   5, 11, 13, 18, 18, 20, 35, 37, 40, 53, 56, 59, 63, 67, 68
Britain and Ireland   30
Brithguein   67
British   38
British Celtic tongues   34
British Isles   13, 22, 34, 37, 38, 38, 39, 44, 51, 58
British Isles as Pretanic   52
British Museum   28
Britons   34
Brittanic Hebraisms   32
Brittonic   52, 60
Brittunculi   59
Bronze Age   40, 43, 46
Bronze Age, Old   43
Brut y Tywysogyon   69
Brynaich   57
Brythonic   4, 4, 18, 24, 40, 52, 52, 52, 53, 55, 60
Brythonic Celtic culture   57
Brythonic kings   68
Bréton   52
Buchanan, George   52
Cadwaladr   69, 71
Cadwallon   70
Caer Drewyn   6, 61, 69, 70
Caer Drewyn hillfort   61
Caernarfon (Segontium)   60
Caernarfon, garrison at   80
Caerwent   60
Cae'r Drewyn   77
Cairnpapple Hill, West Lothian   57

Caledonians	14
Cambridge University	78
Canaanites	30
Cappadocia	21
Carchardy Owain Glyndwr	76
Cardiff	79
Cardigan	79
Cardiganshire	78
Carmarthen	60, 79
Carmarthenshire	78
Carpathian	38
Carrog	62, 75, 76, 76, 79
Carthaginians	37
Caspian Sea	4, 9, 18, 20
Catrin	82
Catrin Glyndwr	83
Catrin, married Sir Edmund Mortimer	82
Catrin, Owain Glyndwr's daughter	78
Caucasian	26
Caucasian Subarian	13
Caucasus	16, 26, 55
Caucasus mountains	9
Caucasus Mountains	11
Caucuses	38
Cein	67
Ceiriog valley	70
Celtic	11, 18, 27, 30, 34, 37, 55, 56, 66
Celtic art	20, 44
Celtic Britain	54
Celtic groups	9, 24
Celtic language	29
Celtic languages	52
Celtic peoples	15
Celtic settlement	58
Celtic tribes of Britain	13
Celts	5
CELTS	7
Celts	7, 10, 11, 16, 21, 21, 22, 22, 34, 39, 43, 43, 55, 61
Celts of Wales	43
Central Asia	38
Central Asian steppes	12
Ceredig	65, 66, 67
Ceredigion	71
Charles Edwards	32, 32
Charles IV of France	80
Charles VI of France	73
Chester	69, 77
Chiltern Hills	13
China	11

Christian church	60
Christina, daughter of Goronwy ap Owain	70
Cilan	77
Cimbri	37, 38
Cimmerian	22
Cimmerians4, 4, 4, 5, 10, 11, 14, 15, 16, 18, 18, 20, 20, 21, 35, 35, 38, 41, 42, 43, 44, 44, 45, 55	
Cirencester	62, 62
Claudius, Emperor	59
Clyde	59, 59
Clyde, river	54
Coel	67
Coel Hen	55
Coel Hen (Old King Cole)	56, 57
Coel Hen Godhebog	68
Colchester	62
comet lit up the skies of North Wales	78
Conway Castle	78
Corded Ware	42, 45
Corded Ware Culture	58
Corded-Ware	41
Cornish	52, 54, 59
Corwen	6, 45, 62, 69, 70, 81, 82
Cotofeni	56
Cremation	43
Cremona	63
Crimea	16
Crogen	77
Crug Mawr	71
Cumberland	18
Cumbria	57, 65
Cumbric	54
Cuneda	67
Cunedd Wledig, (Kuneda Wloedeg)	64
Cunedda	53, 64, 66
Cunedda Wledig	55, 56, 66, 67
Cunedda Wledig	67
Cymru	15, 18
Cymry	38, 65, 65
Cynllaith	73, 74, 75
Cynwyd	70
Czech Republic	47
Czecho-Slovak	27
D.A. MacKenzie	14
Dan Tribe	34
Dan tribe	35
Danube	20, 20, 22, 56
Danube River	22
Danube valley	18

Danube Valley 36, 36
Danube valley 44
David 82
Davidii 13, 38
Davidii 34
Davies, Rees 75
de Montgomerie, Robert 72
Death of Cunedda (poem) 67
Deceangli 62
Dee estuary 71
Dee valley 70
Dee, river 75
Deheubarth 69
Denbigh 77, 78
Denmark 44
Dibun 67
Dillon and Chadwick, linguists 54
Din Eidyn 55, 56
Dineidin 11
Dinmael 77
Diodorus Siculus 37
DNA 48, 49, 50
DNA analysis 10, 47
DNA technology 5
Dogfael 67
Doli 67
Doli ap Gwrddu of Britain 67
Don River 13
Dr John Davies 33, 35
Dr Thomas Moore 29
Dr. Davies 33
Druids 62
Dubun 67
Dukes of the Britons 68
Dumn 67
Dun Breatann (Dumbarton) 65
Dunod 67
Dyffryn Clwyd 70
Earl of Surrey 73, 73
Earl Ranulf of Chester 71
Early Iron Age 42
East Lothian 4, 5, 11
Eburacum (York) 57
Edeirnion 70, 77
Edern 67, 67
Edern ap Padarn (Aeternus) 56
Edeyrnion 4, 4, 5, 5, 6, 43, 45, 52, 61, 61, 62, 74, 75, 75
Edinburgh 4, 11, 55, 65
Edmund Hakluyt 74

Edward I	73
Edward Lhuyd	27
Edwards, Owain M.	82
Egypt	13, 21
Egyptian	34
Egyptians	30
Eimet	67
Einion Yrth	67
Eleanor of Castile	73
Emperor Claudius	62
England	51, 54, 55, 69, 71, 71, 78
Englefield	69
English Maelor	69
Estonia	11
Etruscan	44
Etruscan chariot	44
Eugein	67
Eumenius	14
Eurasia	9
Europe	4, 4, 9, 9, 14, 20, 20, 22, 28, 39, 42, 45, 49, 58
European	12
European Bronze Age	58
Ewein	67
Exeter	62
Exiled Israel	35
Exiles of Isaac	18
Feni	56
Fife	52
Finnish	27
Firth of the Forth	55
Flanders	69
Flint	77, 78
Flintshire	69
Forth	59, 59
Forth, river	52, 53, 54
Foss Way	62
France	40, 44, 50, 54, 78, 79
Frank	36
Franks	11
Franz von Miklosich	27
French	73
Frisia	51
Frisian Islands	51
Funnel Beaker	41
Gadie	13
Gaelic	27, 53
Galatae	37, 38
Galatai	20
Galatia	58
Galatians	37, 37

Galica 18
Galicia 18
Gallic 18
Gamir 19
Gamkrelidze 26
Gascony 69
Gaul 59
Gauls 16, 21, 34
Genedawc 67
Gentes Scitiae 11
Georgia 18
German 27
Germanic 27, 53
Germanic languages 52
Germany 36, 43, 47, 50, 51
Gesoriacum (Boulogne) 59
Gilead 14
Gimirae 17
Gimiri 35
Gimirraja 21
Gloucester 62
Glyndyfrdwy 62, 73, 74, 75, 75, 76, 78
Goidelic 52, 52, 52
Gordoli 67
Gorein 67
Goths 13, 14, 17, 36
Goutodin 56, 56
Goutodin kingdom 55
Grampians 13
Great Britain 54
Greece 34, 35, 60
Greek 24, 27, 44
Greeks 9
Gruffudd ap Cynan 69
Gruffudd ap Madog 73, 73
Gruffudd ap Rhys 71
Gruffudd Fychan 73, 74
Gruffydd 82
Gruffydd ap Cynan 71
Guorcein 67
Guordoli 67
Gurdumn 67
Guti 17
Gwawl verch Coel Hen 67
Gwen 67
Gwladys, daughter of Llywarch 70
Gwynedd 55, 56, 69, 70, 71, 73
Gwynedd 65
Gwynionydd, Cardiganshire 74

Gymrias   19
Haddington in Lothian   56
Hadrian's wall   56, 59
Hadrian's Wall   60
Hadrian's wall   65
Hadrian's Wall   67
Halley's comet   78
Hallstatt   43
Hallstatt Celtic culture   22
Hallstatt culture   42, 58
Halstatt   36, 38
Hamitic   30, 34
Hamito-Semitic   34
Hanmer, Sir David   74
Harlech   78, 79, 79, 80
Harleian Manuscripts of Oxford   81
Harleian MS 3859   67
Harleian MS.   75
Hastings, battle of   78
Haverfordwest   79
Hawkes, Christopher   54
Hebraic   35
Hebrew   5, 13, 18, 32, 35, 37, 38
Hebrew   32
Hebrew and Welsh   33
Hebrews   28, 29
Hebrews   29
Hebrides Islands   37
Helvetti   38
Hendwr   77
Henry II   6, 69, 70, 71
Henry IV   77, 78, 79, 83, 83
Henry, Duke of Lancaster   82
Henry's, Prince - murderous deed   76
Herefordshire   78, 81, 82
heronry   75
Hiberi   37, 37
Hibernia   37
Hilversum culture   46
Himalaya Mountains   9
Hindus   13, 50
Hiraethog mountains   77
Historia Brittonum   67
Historia Regum Britanniae   68
Hittite   30, 30, 34
Hittite kingdom   16
Hittites   9
Holt   77
Homer   37

Homo Ergaster 48
Homo Sapiens Sapiens 48
Hope 69
Hu Gadarn 36
Hugh D'Avranches 72
Hugh of Montgomerie 72
Humber 59
Humphrey, Duke of Gloucester 81
Hungarian 27
Hungary 47
Hurrian 26
Hywel Dda 73
Iago 67
Iberi 38
Iberia 18, 35
Iberians 38
Iceni tribe 62
India 4, 9, 9
Indian subcontinent 4
Indo-European 4, 4, 5, 5, 7, 8, 9, 9, 12, 15, 20, 20, 27, 27, 30, 31, 34, 35, 36, 49, 50, 52, 55, 81
Indo-European expansion 58
Indo-European language 40, 41, 48
Indo-European migration 47
Indo-Europeans 26
Indo-Iranian 10, 24
Indus Valley 4, 4, 4, 16, 17, 50
Iolo Goch 75
Iorwerth Goch ap Maredudd 69
Iran 5, 9, 16, 17, 21, 45
Iranian 15
Iranian-speakers 41
Iranians 19
Iraq 15
Ireland 31, 35, 38, 40, 79
Irish 27, 34, 52, 56
Irish invaders 67
Iron Age people 58
Iron Age, European 44
Isaac 18
Isabel 82
Isle of Man 54, 54
Isqi-Gulu 18
Israel 17, 18, 19, 30, 36, 37
Israelite 13
Israelites 28
Italian 27
Italic 27
Italy 9, 37

Iudeorurn 29
Ivanov 26
Iâl 71
J. P. Mallory 24
J.Morris Jones 30
James Parker 21
Jane 82
Janet 82
Jeaninne Davis-Kimbell 22
Jesus College MS 20 67
John 82
John Henry 21
John le Strange 74
Jorgen Laessoe 21
Joseph, tribes of 38
Judah 29
Judaism 13
Judeorurn 29
Julius Caesar 14
Jutes 29
Keltoi 20
Kent, John (Sion Caint) 75
Khazar 13
Khazars 14
Khumri 35
King Edward II 74
King Gruffudd ap Cynan 70
King Henry V 80, 81
King Sargon 20
Kizil-Koba Colchis 15
Kumayri 19
Kuneda Wloedig ap Edeyrn 66
Kurdistan 26
Kurds 10
L.G.A. Roberts 32
La Tène 43, 43
La Tène Celtic 37
La Tène Celtic culture 22
Lake Leninkan 18
Lake Neûchatel, Switzerland 44
Lake Urmia 5, 18, 21
Lake Van (Eastern Turkey) 16
Late Bronze 42
Latin 54
Lawton's Hope, hill of in Herefordshire 82
Leland, John 76
Lincoln 62
Livingston, Michael 81
Livio Frulovisi, Tito 81
Llansantffraid Glyndyfrdwy 75, 75

Llansilin 75
Llidiart-y-Parc 76, 77
London 62
Longthorpe 62
Lord Grey 77
Lord Grey of Ruthin 77
Lord Grey, taken prisoner 78
Lord Rhys ap Gruffudd 69
Lost Ten Tribes 17, 35, 36
Lost Ten Tribes   of Israel 17
Lothian 52, 53, 55, 64
Lydia 18
Machir of Menasseh 14
Machynlleth 79
Madog 74, 82
Madog ap Idnerth 69
Madog ap Maredudd 69
Mallory, J.P. 48, 48
Manasseh 37
Manau Gododdin 65
Manaw 55
Manaw Gododdin 4, 5, 18, 64
Mannai 5, 21
Mannaie 18
Manx 52
Maredudd 82
Margaret 82
Margaret Hanmer of Flint 82
Margaret, Owain Glyndwr's wife taken prisoner 80
Marija Gimbutas 11
Maximus Magnus 63
Maximus Wledig 56, 64
Medes 10
Media 18
Median Plateau 15
Mediterranean 22, 28, 28
Mediterranean basin 4, 9
Mediterranean culture 60
Mediterranean Sea 20
Megalommitis, Professor 38
Meirion Goch of Llyn 72
Meirionydd 70
Menai Straits 80
Mercia, kingdom of 82
Mesopotamia 4, 4, 9, 15, 16, 17, 17, 26, 45
Mesopotamia (Iraq) 4
Mesopotamian Sumerians 15
Middle-English 81
Minyan pottery 46

Mitanni	30, 34
Moel y Gwynt	70
Monnington	75
Monnington, Herefordshire	81
Monnington, Margaret	81
Mons Graupius	60
Mortimer, Edmund	78
Mortimer, Edmund the 5th Earl of March	83
Mortimer, Edmund, killed	80
Mortimer, Roger	83
Mortimer, Sir Edmundr	83
Mortimers of Chirk	74
Moses, Grace	55
MS Bodley 966	82
MS Harley 35	82
Mycenean Greek	30, 34
Mynyw (Menevia)	29
Mythology of the Ancient Druids	35
Nash Ford, D. and Kessler, Peter L.	68
National Library of Wales	74, 75
Near East	22
Near-Eastern farmers	48
Neaverson, Dr E.A.	76
Nennius	67
neo-Babylonian	35
Neolithic era, late	40
Neolithic tribes	40
Netherlands	46, 50, 51
Nineveh	22, 35
Ninth Legion	62, 62
Nordic-Baltic	20
Norman castle	76
Normandy	69
Normans	71, 78
North Africa	31, 34, 35
North America	38
north of Britain	44
North Pontic	11
North Wales	4, 5, 14
North Wales, King of	66
Northern Britain	55, 56
Northumberland	55
Northumbria	18
Offa's Dyke	78
Old King Cole	5, 68
Old Testament	30
Old Welsh	53
Ordovices	62
Orkney islands	40

Orpheus 37
Oswestry 69, 70, 77
Oumun 67
Owain ap Edwin 70
Owain ap Gruffudd 70
Owain Cyfeiliog 69
Owain Glyndwr 6, 45, 69, 73, 74, 75, 75, 76, 77, 78, 79, 80, 81
Owain Glyndwr - proclaimed Prince of Wales 77
Owain Glyndwr's children 82
Owain Glyndwr, The Rebellion of 77
Owain Glyndwr's death 82
Owain Gwynedd 6, 69, 70
Oxford University 78
Oxygen Isotope Analysis 47
O'Rahilly, R.F. 54
p-Celtic 52
Padarn ap Tegid (Paternus 56
Padarn Beisrud 67
Padarn Beisrudd 67
Padarn Beisrudd (Paturnus of the Red Cloak) 66
Pakistan 4, 10
Palestine 28, 28
Panton Manuscript 75
Parthians 10
Patern Pesrut 67
Paternus 67
Paternus' Red-Robe 67
Peniarth Manuscript 74
Pennant, Thomas 76
Penybont farm 77
Percy, Earl of Northumberland 78
Persia 9
Persia (Iran) 4
Persian 11
Persians 10
Peter Ellis 20
Phoenician 28
Phoenician-Celtic ties 29
Phoenicians 28
Pictish 52, 53
Pictish culture 53
Pictish stone carvings 45
Picts 4, 10, 11, 13, 14, 24, 55, 59
Pit Grave Culture 45, 45
Plantagenet monarchy 71
Polish 27
Pontic Bosporus 16
Pontic Steppes 15
Pontic steppes 36, 41
Pontic/Russian steppes 14

Pontus 11
Portugal 40
Powys 69, 71
Powys, dynasty of 78
Prince Hal 79
Prince Madog ap Maredydd 71
Prince of Northern Powys 6
Prince of Wales 78
Proto-Brythonic 58
Proto-Indo-European 24
Proto-Indo-European language 9
Proto-Indo-European Language Links 23
Proto-Indo-Europeans 17
Prydain 52
Prydein 67
Ptolemy 37
Pyfog of Ireland 70
Pyrenees 38
Pytheas of Massilia 52
q-Celtic 52
Quarietii 54
Queen Eleanor 74
Radnorshire 78
Red Robe ap Tegid 67
Red Sea 42
Reginald de Grey of Ruthin 74
Renfrew, Colin 48
Rev. Eliezer Williams 34
Rhagad (Rhagatt) 76
Rhagatt Hall 76
Rheged 68
Rhine 20, 20
Rhine region 44
Rhone 20, 20
Rhos 70
Rhuddallt 75, 75
Rhuddlan 69, 77
Rhufon 67
Rhufoniog 70
Richard II 82
River Gade 13
Roger Mortimer of Chirk 73
Roman 18, 62
Roman Britain 57, 68
Roman conquest 43
Roman Duces Drittanniarum 57
Roman Empire 44, 61
Roman military 56
Roman occupation 54
Roman papacy, withdrawal of support for 80

Romanian	27
Romanized British tribes	60
Romano-British farmer	60
Romans	5, 5, 11, 18, 55, 57, 59, 59, 61, 62, 68
Romany language	27
Rome	56, 60, 63
Royal Asiatic Society of Bengal	27
Royal Commission on ancient monuments	82
Rug	72, 77
Rug Hall	71
Russia	13, 20, 39
Russian	27
Russian steppe	4, 10
Russian Steppe	49
Russian Steppes	45
Ruthin	77, 77, 78
Salzburg	42
Samarians	15
Samuel Lysons	21
Sanskrit	5, 27, 30, 34
Sarmatians	11
Saxon	11, 55
Scandinavia	35
Scandinavian	27, 36
Scotland	4, 5, 11, 13, 45, 54, 55, 55, 59, 64, 65, 69, 77, 79, 79, 80
Scottish	27, 34, 53
Scottish countryside	40
Scottish Gaelic	52
Scudamore	75
Scudamore, Alice	81
Scythia	11, 13
Scythian	11, 16, 18, 44, 55
Scythian/Cimmerian	44
Scythians	4, 5, 10, 10, 11, 14, 15, 17, 20, 21, 21, 22, 37, 38
Scyths	36
Seine	20
Semitic	34, 35
Semitic (Hebrew)	30
Sennacherib	22
Serbo-Croatian	27
Severn	59
Severn, river	62
Sforza, Cavill	50, 50
Shaul, (Silures of South Wales)	38
Shrewsbury	70, 72, 77, 79
Sidonius Apollinaris	14
Silures	62
Simeon	38
Sir Austen Henry Layard	28

Sir John Rhys	29
Sir William Jones	27
Slavic	27
Slavs	10
Solway Firth	60
Spain	9, 37, 40, 60, 63, 79
Spanish	27
St Albans	63, 74
St David's	29
St Mael and St Sulien	6
St Mael and St Sulien Church, Corwen	81
St Mael and St Sulien, Corwen	75
Statute of Rhuddlan of 1284	73
Steppe area, Ukraine	45
Steppes of Europe	4, 4, 4
Stirling	55
Stonehenge	29
Strabo	16
Strathclyde	65
Strathspey	53
Strontium Isotope Analysis	47
Suetonius	62
Suetonius Paulinus	61
Sumeria	4, 4, 24
Sumerian	5, 26
Switzerland	44
Sycharth	75, 76, 79
Sykes, Bryan	49, 50, 50
Syria	18, 60
Syrian	30, 34
Tacit	67
Tacitus	67
Taliesin	35
Tamara Talbot Rice	20
Tatarstan	41
Tegeingl	67, 69, 71
Tegid ap Cein (Tacitus)	56
Tegyth	67
Telford, Thomas	76
Ten Lost tribes of Israel	38
Ten Tribes	21
Ten Tribes of Israel	38
Tenby	79
Teushpa	35
Teutons	10, 39
Thomas	82
Thomas of Macclesfield	74
Thomas V. Gamkrelidze	9
Thracian	24

Thracian-Sumerian	15
Thraco-Cimmerian	16
Tiglathpileser III	35
Titus Maccius Plautus	29
Tocharia	9
Towcester	63
Traprain Law	55, 57
Trewyn, Corwen	61
Tribes of Israel	37
Tudur ap Gruffudd	74, 76
Tudur ap Gryffudd	77
Tungrians	59
Turkestan	9
Turkey	9, 41
Tweed, river	57
Tybion	67
Tyne, river	55, 57, 60
Tènian culture	44
Ukraine	4, 15, 36
Umbria	18
University College, London	51
Urartian	26
Urartu	18, 18, 22
Urnfield	43
Urnfield Culture	36, 58
Urnfields	43
V.V. Ivanov	9
Vale of Clwyd	77
Valentia	57
Van Loon	18
Vedic	30, 34
Vindolanda	59
Virgil	5
Vita Henrici Quinti - biography of Henry V	81
Vortigern	64, 66
Vortigern (Wyrtgeorn)	56
Votadini	4, 4, 5, 10, 14, 55, 56, 57, 60
Votadini Celts	64
Votadini tribe	53, 67
Votadini tribes	52
W.H.Worrell	30
Wales	15, 18, 24, 31, 35, 38, 40, 44, 51, 56, 57, 60, 61, 62, 66, 73, 78, 79, 80
Wales, flag of	38
Wales, North	41, 53, 55, 56, 62, 63, 64, 65, 67, 69, 77
Wales, South	71, 74
Walter Baucum	34, 35
Wash, the	62
Watling Street	62
Welsh	11, 27, 27, 32, 34, 34, 38, 52, 53, 54, 55, 59

Welsh army	6
Welsh Brythonic tribe	46
Welsh kings	68
Welsh language	5, 9, 9
Welsh, Old	53
Welshpool	77, 78
Westminster	74, 75
Williams, Gwyn A.	52, 56
Williams, Gwyn A.	58
Wittlewood	63
Y chromosones	50
Y Gododdin	11
Yair Davidii	5, 11, 17, 34, 37
Yorkshire	59
Ysfael Gwron	67
Zoomorphic Juncture	45
"Glas"	31

CELTS: LONG JOURNEY TO WALES
© Dennis Wyn Williams 2005 – 2016

Printed in Poland
by Amazon Fulfillment
Poland Sp. z o.o., Wrocław